Praise for *Vitamin C for a He[...]*

"This book will meet 100 percent of your daily requirement for nurturing management wisdom. Comprehensive. Conceptually sound. Constructively positive."

Ian Percy
Author of The 7 Secrets to a Life of Meaning *and* Going Deep

"Most leadership 'gurus' either oversimplify a complex process or use difficult-to-understand terminology to teach it. Joe and Luke have successfully 'walked that fine line' that explains complicated leadership issues in everyday language."

Allan Stewart, MBA
President, Human Synergistics Canada

"A superb guide which will inspire your courage and help you discover the environment where you can align your passion with your profession."

Robin Sharma, Professional Speaker
Author of The Monk Who Sold His Ferrari

"This powerful, practical book gives you a series of proven techniques to build a high-performance workplace. It is worth its weight in gold."

Brian Tracy
Internationally Renowned Speaker

"If you don't find inspiration and information you can use in this book, you just aren't paying attention."

Glen Morehouse, AOCA
GRAPHUS Advertising

"The formula for organizational success has never been so clearly stated."

Joe Pavelka
Author of It's Not About Time!
Rediscovering leisure in a changing world

"Simply stated, *Vitamin C for a Healthy Workplace* is important, comprehensive and yet fun to read."

Alan Middleton, Director
Schulich School of Business, York University

"The great thing about 'Vitamin C', is that you can't get too much. It is also impossible to have too many people in your organization who have read this book. If everyone has taken this 'Vitamin C', you will have a healthier workplace."

Warren Evans, Business Trends Expert
President, The Service Excellence Group Inc.

Vitamin C for a Healthy Workplace

Luke De Sadeleer
& Joseph Sherren

Resources for personal growth and enhanced performance
www.creativebound.com

ISBN 0-921165-73-0
Printed and bound in Canada

Book design by Wendelina O'Keefe

Printing number 10 9 8 7 6 5 4 3

Canadian Cataloguing in Publication Data

De Sadeleer, Luke
    Vitamin C for a healthy workplace

Includes bibliographical references.
ISBN 0-921165-73-0

1. Success in business. 2. Job satisfaction. I. Sherren, Joseph
II. Title.

HF5549.D436 2001   650.1   C2001-903105-X

Dedicated to the memory of

PETER T. ZARRY
1933 – 2001

Director, Schulich School of Business
York University

A great leader and friend who is truly missed.

Acknowledgments

First, thanks must go to all the people who have attended our seminars, asked thought-provoking questions, and shared their personal experiences in the workplace. This has provided invaluable fodder from which we are able to develop current and relevant programs and book material.

Also, thank you to Human Synergistics for allowing us to use their instrumentation and survey material used by many corporations and organizations. These include: Stylus, Life Styles Inventory, Organizational Culture Inventory, Group Styles Inventory and the Management Effectiveness Profile System.

We appreciate Gail Baird, Lindsay Pike, Barb Clarke and Jill Grassie at Creative Bound Inc., book publishers, for being great mentors and providing us with guidance throughout this process. Special thanks to editor Brenda Stewart and book designer Wendy O'Keefe.

Another thank you to the Canadian Association of Professional Speakers (CAPS). As an organization they are both encouraging and supportive to people who want to find their passion in the professional speaking industry. It was also the venue where we first met and explored the possibility of a synergistic relationship.

We would also like to mention motivational speakers with whom we have worked and who have inspired us in the past, among those: Ian Percy, Brian Tracey, Dr. Alex Horniman, Dr. Gerry Cusack and Norm Rebin.

Most special thanks to Susan Olsen, Joe's director of operations, who managed his schedule, provided client relations, ran his business and kept us organized. She also kept us focused on the task of writing this book. Her many hours of dedication to compiling and organizing information made it possible to meet the deadlines required. She was also instrumental in the initial editing and arranging of the thought sequences in this book.

Joe would like to single out his wonderful wife, P.J., who was (as always) supportive and understanding while he chased another one of his dreams.

He also appreciated the encouragement, direction and friendship—while considering whether to begin this project—from Elaine Gutmacher, who is the associate director at York University's Schulich School of Business.

Luke would like to thank his loving wife, Susan, for her continued support and inspiration during the writing of this book.

Foreword

By Alan Middleton Ph.D.
Director, Executive Education
Division of Executive Development
Schulich School of Business, York University, Toronto, Canada

The formula for organizational success is clear. Be the very best at employing, training, organizing, rewarding and motivating those who work for you and with you. Simple huh? So why are we still agonizing over how to do this well?

Well, of course, it is not that simple and never has been. In fact it has become a lot more difficult. In a globally competitive environment where competition is faster and better organized than ever before, and where customers and consumers are smarter and more demanding than ever before, the 'right' solutions are neither as evident nor as obviously right. Add to this the fact that employees are no longer content to be workaholic 'drones', and most important, that we no longer want them to be. Then, we begin to understand that while it is so easy to *say*, "be the best at employing, training, organizing, rewarding and motivating," it is very difficult to *do*.

The popular business press is full of articles about inverted organizational triangles, self-managing teams, competency analyses and the never-ending concepts and jargon of business literature. But have we really become any wiser in our practices? We will not while we hop from one faddish idea to another.

Improvement in the use of this most valuable resource, human talent, comes from logic, intuition, understanding, an ability to listen yet be decisive and, perhaps most of all, from learning and experience.

This book explores the learning and experience in this area. It examines the keys to getting and keeping talented people. It shows us how to assess individuals, and how to develop successful and healthy teams. Very importantly, it helps us to assess ourselves and our own strengths and weaknesses as colleagues and leaders.

Vitamin C for a Healthy Workplace aids us in developing paths of continuous learning and improvement such that we can better handle the rapid changes of the business environment. Like Vitamin C, it does not suggest that it is a magic potion for everlasting health, but rather that continuous exposure will improve our health and help us withstand assaults on it.

The authors give us a comprehensive overview of sensible and actionable analyses that we can apply to ourselves, our teams and our workplace in general. They make this overview readable, approachable and actionable.

Simply stated, *Vitamin C for a Healthy Workplace* is important, comprehensive and yet fun to read. Working to apply their principles, to take a regular dose of Vitamin C will result in a healthier workplace for you—one that is more productive, more creative and more fun.

We are finally beginning to notice that both children and adults learn better when they enjoy it. It is a simple yet fundamental concept, but we very often forget it.

The authors of this book have not.

Enjoy it.

Contents

Introduction

How *Vitamin C for a Healthy Workplace* Will Help You

Imagine a workplace where you have no problem retaining your star performers. Picture also an environment where your employees do what they love to do, and one that supports and encourages the development of their strengths. Impossible? Not at all. As this book will show you, it's all about energy, passion and the right attitude.

Let's face it, retention management is a buzzword of the new millennium. We also know that what makes people stay with an organization is not only about money. It is about creating a healthy work environment that contributes to the well-being of all individuals.

In today's competitive environment it is extremely important to remember that it is the "people" who are critical to an organization's success. That means doing more than giving lip service to the adage, "People are our number one resource." By actually demonstrating the principle in its operations, an organization can harness the collective potential of all of its employees and create a highly powerful force against its competitors.

The best organizations know how to keep their top performers. They are aware that the competition would love to steal their top talent, and they know they simply can't afford to lose these valuable people. Executives of these organizations understand that one of the best ways to achieve retention is to create a balance between the goals of the employees and the goals of the business.

Vitamin C for a Healthy Workplace provides a prescription for aligning the passion of the people with the mission of the organization. The prescription consists of seven "C"s. These are: **Change, Career, Culture, Coaching, Communication, Conflict** and **Connection**. Each of the seven "C"s represents a principle to accelerate organizational growth and productivity by developing employees and managers who are passionate about their work.

This book also addresses three areas of responsibility for creating a healthy workplace:

1. *The individual provides the energy.*
2. *The manager provides the coaching.*
3. *The organization provides the environment.*

How to Take *Vitamin C for a Healthy Workplace*

The information presented in this book comes from our own experience working with people and organizations, combined with case studies and research. You will discover that we believe very strongly in the value of a healthy workplace and, further, that organizations must do whatever is necessary to create this supportive environment.

We realize that you may not agree with everything we suggest or believe. That's fine. Please feel free to choose those areas that mean the most to you. Use what works best for your situation.

Each chapter of this book builds on the previous one. Therefore, to get the most from this book, we suggest that you read the chapters in order. However, you may also find that specific chapters relate more to you than others. If this is the case, you might want to scan them all first to see which are more relevant to your interests.

Finally, to help you determine the status of your present environment, you will also find self-awareness exercises in each chapter.

Putting the seven "C"s into practice will result in a healthy workplace where you are doing what you love to do, and doing it in an environment that supports and encourages the development of your strengths.

Change

Change Gears or Get Shifted!

**Growth means change and change involves risks,
stepping from the known to the unknown.**
George Shinn

What's Changing?

Everything we read indicates that we all are experiencing more rapid change than at any other time in history. As authors who have studied the workplace extensively, we are here to tell you that this is absolute cow patty—nothing has really changed at all! Where change comes from. How we deal with it. Why we fear it. These questions have remained the same since Adam and Eve had to adjust to a new neighborhood.

Most of us have heard the saying "The only constant is change." Did you also know it was said, many centuries ago, by the Greek philosopher Heraclitus? The fact is, we have been told, for millennia, how quickly our lives are changing.

So what changes are we dealing with *today* that are causing people to add stress to their lives? Let's reflect on some of them.

- The amount of information in a single issue of the *New York Times* is comparable to that which a person of the 16th century would have assimilated throughout a lifetime. Available information in the year 2000 was doubling at a rate of more than every five years. By 2010, it will double every six months. By 2035, it will double every 30 minutes.
- Experts believe that people entering the workforce today can expect to change careers up to five times in their lifetimes.
- Students entering a four-year university program can expect that the profession or career for which they are studying will have changed significantly by the time they graduate. In some cases it will have even become obsolete.
- In this technological age, the boundaries to what we can create are becoming fewer and fewer.
- Unconditional lifetime employment is gone forever.

The world of work has been redefined by empowerment, self-managed teams, re-engineering, independent contractors and virtual corporations. We are all trying to understand and respond to the changes occurring in our workplace and personal lives. At times we feel overwhelmed, but we humans are adaptable folks. We have been adjusting to change since being able to stand up and walk on two feet.

When it comes to our careers, times continue to change. Many of us are no longer looking myopically at traditional job opportunities. We are looking inwardly, at ourselves, to see what we can create. Gone are the days when many of us grew up and were told, "Go to school and get good marks. If you get good marks you'll pass, and if you pass twelve or thirteen times in a row you'll graduate. If you graduate, you go knock on someone's door, and say give me a job. You'll work there for 20 or 30 years. At the end they'll give you a gold watch, and then you'll retire."

In today's reality most of us will not stay in the same company, or job, very long. Employers are now telling us that many of them are thinking of keeping you for three years; beyond that there is no guarantee. The rationale is that a three-year time span gives them enough time to recover the costs incurred during the hiring process.

How we are going to have to work in the future is different than how we have worked in the past. Even Einstein prepared his students for dealing with change. When asked why he used the same exam questions as the previous year, Einstein replied, "because the answers have all changed."

Like it or not, change has always been a part of our lives, and we can predict with a fair degree of certainty that it always will be.

Why Change?

It is important that we react to change in a positive and productive manner. Downsizing, rightsizing, restructuring, re-engineering, revitalizing—whatever the business term—millions of people are eventually finding themselves in a new world of work where they must adapt to a new way of thinking.

We are all too familiar with the shifts in the marketplace and the impact on people in the workplace. Employers are looking for "value added." They are thirsting for solution-oriented individuals who can help them solve a problem or improve their operations.

Today's successful businesses are those that are moving to flexible, customer-focused and proficient positions, taking advantage of the rapidly changing business environment. In order to achieve it, everyone involved must bring more value than cost.

In many of these restructured organizations, people are fortunate enough to find themselves in a growing environment, but with that comes the fact that they must learn new skills. No longer is doing the same old stuff good enough. They must learn to be entrepreneurs, contributing to the organization they work for as if it were their own. We call them *intrepreneurs*, those who provide measurable, added value.

Many organizations have also learned that to succeed, they must harness the collective potential of all their employees. By doing this, they will create the most powerful force against their competitors. But it involves teamwork.

Unfortunately, the journey to employees working as a cohesive team is fraught with difficulties. Executives resist, because it appears they will lose control. Employees resist, figuring the switch is just another fleeting passion for management people with too much time on their hands.

The contract between employees and employers has been rewritten, and the ways that employees work together must be more synergistic. Everyone in the organization must be educated in the ways these rules have changed. As our friend Jim Clemmer states in his excellent book, *Growing the Distance,* "The popular goals of security, stability, and predictability are deadly. The closer we get to these dangerous goals, the more our growth is stunted and learning reduced. In today's fast-changing world, if we fail to change, it is we who will be changed."

A company's very survival and long-term success depends on how quickly and efficiently its people respond to change.

Are People Able to Adapt to All This Change?

The answer is a resounding yes! However, it will take a desire to grow both mentally and emotionally. This book will cover the emotional dimension more extensively in a later chapter.

From an intellectual standpoint, researchers tell us that we use a very small portion of our brain's capacity. Although there are differing opinions on exactly how much, most agree that we are still operating in the first one-tenth percentile of its total potential.

They now know that people who do exercise their brains live longer, are less susceptible to Alzheimer's, and stay healthier than people who do not. There is much evidence to this fact. All you have to do to see examples is look at people who did exercise their brains or wit consistently during their lives, and think about how long they lived. Think about people such as Einstein, Alexander Graham Bell, Edison, Bob Hope, Johnny Carson and George Burns.

The secret that these people all learned was that in order to maintain a healthy outlook on life, they had to take control of their own lives within the constant environment of change. They also learned to remain on a quest for constant learning and personal growth.

The fact is, people actually DO like change. People create their own change all the time. They change their clothes, their cars, their jobs, their houses and, many times, even their spouses. The issue is that people don't like *being* changed.

Each of us must realize that the rate of change in the world is not going to slow down. Consequently, we must develop strategies to help us maintain a sense of personal control in such an environment. When we are able to accomplish that stance, we will look forward to life and the future with enthusiasm, optimism and joy.

Why Do Most People Resist the Opportunity to Grow?

The answer in many ways is complex; however, on the surface there are some very pragmatic reasons. Here are some of the common ones:

- a fear of the unknown;
- a vested interest in the status quo;
- a fear of failure, or a fear of success;
- change is inconvenient;
- a lack of trust;

- the possible threat to our livelihood.

Too often we cling desperately to the past. We feel secure in our tried and true, comfortable routines. We staunchly believe in that old saying, "If it ain't broke, don't fix it."

Change is seen as both frightening and enlightening. We are all in a prison of our paradigms. Our colleague, Bill Clennan, a dynamic speaker from Canada's west coast, asks a thought-provoking question: **"If you were born in a prison and did not know you were there, how would you ever know that you should escape?"**

Over the years our minds have been programmed to look at the world a certain way, and to see others a certain way. More importantly, we see ourselves through these same filters. Those views are something we all learn to live with.

But we must escape. Later on in this chapter, we will use a few metaphors from the animal jungle to illustrate some of the similarities to behaviors in the corporate jungle.

The Six Phases of Change

Organizational experts have for many years described predictable phases that people experience as they respond to unexpected change. One of the preeminent authorities on change and managing change is Dr. William Bridges. In his book *Managing Transitions: Making the Most of Change,* Dr. Bridges states, "It isn't the changes that do you in, it's the transition. Change is not the same as transition. *Change* is situational: the new site, the new boss, the new team roles, and the new policy. *Transition* is the psychological process people go through to come to terms with the new situation."

In our experience, working with individuals and organizations, we have seen this transition first-hand. It consists of some predictable phases that individuals usually experience during the transition from an ending to a new beginning.

We have also come to accept that in order to make transition easier it is important to understand these predictable phases. Understanding is necessary for people to feel comfortable with the transition. Understanding and assimilation will allow them to react appropriately.

Managers should understand these phases as well. If employees are not permitted to experience these predictable reactions, the transition process will be prolonged. Employees may even get stuck in one of the phases.

The six *phases of change*, adapted by us over the years, can be identified as follows.

Not me!

The first phase in the transition process is typically called *denial*. We call this the *not me* phase. During this phase, people say or think, "There must be some mistake," "I don't believe it. This can't be happening to me," or something similar. People may experience a sense of numbness.

Some employees behave as if the event has not happened and continue to work assuming things will eventually return to normal. They often stay focused on the way things were, and are reluctant to explore what or how they need to change.

Not everyone will respond in this predictable manner. Some employees may experience what we call the *lucky me* phase. They actually welcome the change, and experience a sense of relief that the hard times are finally over.

It is important that people do not confuse the *not me* phase with the *lucky me* phase. At times they may delude themselves into believing that everything is just fine, when they are actually afraid to face the change.

Why me?

During the second phase people will begin to experience anger. We call this the *why me* phase. They may find themselves using harsh words or being critical of their organization and colleagues. They tend to say things like, "I'll get even," or "This is not fair. Why is this happening to me?"

This is the phase during which people start to react. The adrenaline starts to flow, and they begin to experience a feeling of rebellion. Managers and employees alike should encourage everyone to be open to, and express, their negative feelings. Sharing feelings of anger will allow this phase to progress faster.

Deal with me!

The third phase usually finds people trying to negotiate some kind of deal to either reverse the change or to make it less painful. During the *deal with me* phase they might say, "I'll treat everyone better," "I'll become a better person. I'll even go to church regularly." Those people faced with a job change will frequently say such things as, "I'll take a lesser position," or "I'll take a cut in pay."

During times of organizational downsizing, or when companies take away offices and put employees into cubicles, we often observe this behavior. Employees will try and negotiate, using possibilities they would not have even considered in the past.

They are trying to make some kind of bargain, because they are still resisting the change.

Oh me!

As people enter the fourth phase they will begin to experience a sense of sadness. In the *oh me* phase they will find themselves brooding and feeling discouraged. Some may have low energy and have difficulty sleeping. They have entered a mourning process that allows them to begin to reflect on what is happening.

These phases are often referred to as healing stages. It is important to note that this *oh me* phase actually forces us to slow down and think. It allows people to reflect on what has really happened and how their lives have been affected.

This phase is also the time when people will begin to think about the future.

Now me!

At this point, people have passed the low point and have moved towards the positive side of the curve. In the *now me* phase people recognize the inevitable. They may find themselves asking, "Where do I go from here?" They are beginning to understand how they can turn this change into a new and better opportunity. They accept that it is time to get on with life and are ready to move ahead.

As employees enter the *now me* phase they often create new bonds with co-workers, and search for new ways to relate to each other.

It's up to me!

Good news for those experiencing change. They have entered the sixth and final phase. The *it's up to me* phase finds people moving ahead and setting goals. They are now comfortable with focusing on the future and are choosing a strategy for dealing with it.

People have developed new support systems and are likely creating action plans to put the change to work.

Where Are My Car Keys?

To see a vivid illustration of the phases, remember a time when you were in a rush to go somewhere and found that you had locked the keys in your car. Immediately, you went into the *not me* phase. You searched your pockets or purses, looked around the ground, denying subconsciously that you did in fact leave the keys in the ignition.

Joe describes how he actually observed these phases in action one time while sitting on the deck of his cottage. A neighbor came out of his cottage, got into his mini-van, started the engine, and then returned to his cottage to retrieve an item. When he returned, he discovered that he had locked the keys in the vehicle. His first reaction was of course denial, or *not me*. Searching his pockets for another set of keys, he came up empty. Shaking his head, he was probably thinking, "this can't be happening to me."

His next reaction was anger. He kicked the tires and banged on the roof of the car. Joe even heard him say, among some unprintable expletives, "*Why me!*"

After this passed, the neighbor put his hands in the air in a praying position and said, "I will go to church this Sunday, please just open the doors."

When his *deal with me* failed to produce a desired outcome, the neighbor seemed go into a form of depression. With the keys still in the ignition and firmly locked in the car, he walked over to his cottage and sat on the steps, head down and staring at the ground. He seemed to lose his enthusiasm and was thinking, *oh me*.

Joe was just walking over to offer his help when he saw his neighbor get up and start walking to towards him. He seemed more energized and determined. Typical of the *now me* stage.

Within a short time they came up with some ideas. One was to drive to the home of another neighbor who had a tow truck, and who might have the tools to open the vehicle. Together they got in Joe's car and returned, not only with the proper tool but also with the person who knew how to use it.

The sixth stage, *it's up to me*, was actually facilitated by Joe when he made some suggestions to avoid this problem in the future. The neighbor returned later that day with an extra set of keys and a magnetic key holder. He had devised a strategy (placing this magnetic key container inside the wheel well of the car) that would allow him to access these spare keys if he ever lost or locked his keys inside the car.

That evening, sitting on Joe's deck, they reflected on what happened. His neighbor explained how he had learned a lesson, had grown a little and felt secure about being prepared for the future.

This is what change is all about. We must go through the phases and grow. We will be smarter for the experience.

Managing the Phases

An important point we want to make is that it is normal to go through these phases. It is OK to deny. It is OK to get angry. It is OK to negotiate, and it is OK to be slightly depressed. In fact, it is not only normal but also healthy for you to go through these phases.

A good manager will recognize the fact and support employees passing through each of these phases. However, what is not OK is to get stuck in any one of these phases for an extended period of time. Have you ever worked with anyone who was angry for years, or depressed for months?

In times of significant change it would be wise to help yourself through each of these phases and also support others in a positive way. You can do this by connecting with others who are going through the same experience and want to see the light at the end. Doing this will reduce stress, keep you productive and help you maintain constructive attitudes and behaviors.

Receiving support and bestowing support on others will help you move on to the next phase. As you enter the *now me* phase, you recognize the inevitable, try to make sense of what has happened and then get on with life.

During this phase people must develop their support systems, create a strategy and decide on two things. First, how you are going to get out of this dilemma. Second, what you are going to do to be prepared in case it ever happens again. **You can count on it happening again, and you must develop a strategy so you are prepared when it does.**

Resistance Is Futile!

The *Star Trek* series made the above comment famous. The "Borg" species uses the phrase whenever one of them senses resistance from a species its members are attempting to assimilate. The Borg simply inform them that there is no point in struggling because it won't make any difference.

We mention it here to highlight the valuable lesson it illustrates. How often do we find ourselves struggling with and resisting something that we simply cannot change? Unfortunately, many of us will answer "too often." Usually our response is to rely on our old coping skills or to just try a little harder. If the truth were to be told about whether or not that approach has worked for us in the past, we'd have to say, "Well obviously not, considering the escalation in our stress levels."

The famous coach Vince Lombardi once said, "Just because you're doing something wrong, doing it more intensely isn't going to help." Beating your head against a brick wall is not going to hurt the wall, but it will surely cause you pain. Sometimes the only answer is to find your inner peace and not try to control something over which you have no control. Perhaps it will be helpful to remind ourselves about the well-known serenity prayer, "God grant me the *serenity* to accept the things I cannot change, the *courage* to change the things I can, and the *wisdom* to know the difference."

At times, the best, if not the only, way to handle a situation is to stop struggling. The sayings, "Go with the flow," or "Don't push the river," illustrate perfectly. Just remember, you may think of yourself as a rock or a dam, but it doesn't matter, because no matter how hard you try to stop it, the river will find a way around you.

We find that kind of resistance to changing technologies very similar among different people—especially in areas such as the Internet, e-mail and e-commerce. When we tell them that soon they will all be purchasing goods regularly from the Internet, many say, "not me." But they will be. The reason people are not doing it yet is because we all are just at the tip of the iceberg in terms of technological capabilities.

To get a sense of where we are technologically with computer equipment today, think back to what cars were like in early 1900s. Back then, a new car typically came with a white coat and a set of tools. Just to start it you would put on the white coat, turn the key to the on position, advance the spark, open up the engine bonnet and squeeze a rubber tube that would put gas in the carburetor. Then, you would go to the front with a handcrank, and you would crank the engine until it started. Then you would run back and retard the spark before it backfired too many times or stalled. That was what was required just to start the car. Today we have these little buttons we press from about 50 feet away and the car starts. That is only one example of the way computer technology is evolving.

We will soon have refrigerators automatically ordering our groceries, microwaves reading bar codes to determine cooking times, and cars with systems that determine service problems and automatically book appointments with dealerships to get them repaired. Many of us are being dragged kicking and screaming into the future. Ask yourself…"why?"

The Pain of Changing

The fact is that, for most of us, change is not easy. Working in the area, we have come to believe in the following truism: "When the pain of changing becomes less than the pain of staying the same, people will then be motivated to change." It's worth reminding you, however, that most of us will continue to resist change. It is only when the situation becomes too painful that people begin to accept the fact they would be better off if they did change.

On occasion, people may have wanted a change in their job or working relationship but haven't done anything about it because of fear. Most of us are afraid of the unknown, and prefer the familiar.

How many people do you know, including yourself, who are in situations that are unpleasant? They remain stuck because they fear that the effort required to make the change is more painful than the situation they currently face. It is not until the situation gets too painful that they are motivated to change.

Clearly these people can make change occur if a situation becomes too painful. Wouldn't it be better, though, if people were motivated to change because the experience led to more joy? Then people would say, "When the pleasure of changing became greater than the pleasure of staying the same, we would welcome the change." Whether one defines change as easy or difficult, it is necessary.

Get yourself unstuck and take a chance! After all, as Ellen Glasglow, a Virginia novelist and Pulitzer prize winner, said, "The only difference between a rut and a grave…is in their dimensions." Find out what you are truly afraid of, and what you are assuming may happen.

A few years ago there was a Blue Jays' baseball game on television. Ricky Henderson had made it to first base. As was typical of him, he kept taking his foot off first base and trying to steal second. After doing this a few times, the pitcher saw him and quickly threw the ball to the first baseman and he was out.

One of the TV sports announcers was quick to criticize and say, "There goes Henderson again, getting put out because he took his foot off first base trying to steal second. He gets put out on first more often than any other player." The second announcer said, "Yes, but you have to remember a couple of things. One is he also steals second base more often than any other player, and the second thing is, Henderson has learned that you never get to second until you take your foot off first."

That is what many people are reluctant to do in life—take their foot off first base to go after their dream. But just like Ricky Henderson, they have to realize there will be risk and go for it anyway.

Change will happen when you allow yourself to imagine that, in the end, the change will be positive and less painful than current reality.

Metaphors for Resistance to Change

Organizational psychologists have for many years been attempting to compare animal behavior with human behavior, searching for a link between the animal jungle and the corporate jungle. The studies they conducted have resulted in many interesting findings that, in turn, have been used to explain the human side of change. Some have been especially helpful in illustrating our resistance to change.

In his book *The Babinski Reflex*, Philip Goldberg cites a number of these studies that authors, management consultants, corporate trainers and motivational speakers, just to name a few, use as metaphors for resistance to change. Three of our favorites are as follows.

The Monkey's Dilemma

Researchers went to South America to discover why a particular species of monkeys had become extinct. Not long after beginning their studies they were able to determine that it was the oldest species that had died off, while a number of the younger or newer species still survived.

As researchers delved into the reasons for this situation, they were able to determine some contributory factors. One was that local people had for many years hunted and captured these monkeys in order to sell them to any interested buyer. Another factor was the manner in which they were being captured, coupled with the older monkeys' inability to adapt and change.

During the hunting process, hunters would put food in the knotholes of trees. The monkeys would be attracted to this food and squeeze their hands into the knothole to grab the food. Unfortunately for the monkeys, as they put their hands around the food, causing them to form a fist, they were not able to remove their hand from the hole and retrieve the desired food. The diameter of their fists around the food was now larger than the knothole they had forced their hands into, and they were stuck as long as they refused to let go of the food. The monkeys that did not let go of the food were, of course, captured.

Now you have to realize that this species of monkey had been surviving in this jungle for thousands of years—through drought, hurricanes, floods, famines and hard times. When food was very, very scarce, the only way they stayed alive was by finding food, such as eggs and insects, in the knotholes of the trees. These rare food sources were often the only nourishment they could find to allow them to survive. Consequently, whenever these same monkeys came across the food hidden in the knotholes, they were unwilling to let go. In the newer species of monkeys, some learned to let go and got away. Their ability to adapt and change allowed them to survive as a species. Unfortunately the older species, because of their years of history and conditioning, was unable to learn the new behavior. As a result, they were all captured, and now they're extinct.

In our work with organizations, we find that something similar has happened to many people as well. The good news is that at the moment, they are all relatively successful. The bad news is, if they keep on doing what they've always done they will become extinct.

We have often heard these successful and highly motivated people say, "Yeah, but I'm not one of these old monkeys. I think differently, and I've come in here with some different ideas." Historically, however, these same people have too often succumbed to the survival syndrome and have conformed to the inertia of tradition.

The Pike Syndrome

People who fish know that the best way to catch a pike is to use little fish, or a lure that resembles little fish, for bait. Some creative researchers used this aggressive species in one of their experiments.

The researchers put a number of pike in a large aquarium and then threw in little fish, such as minnows. Predictably, the pike went though the tank like "Pac" men and ate all the little fish. Then the researchers put some minnows into a bell jar and lowered it into the aquarium. As soon as the still-hungry pike saw the little fish, they immediately swam towards them, in order to devour the delectable morsels. To their surprise, they'd bonk their noses on an invisible barrier. They couldn't see the glass. All they knew was that every time they went to eat the fish, they'd end up with sore noses. After many unsuccessful and frustrating attempts to satisfy their hunger, the pike simply gave up. They stopped trying to get at the fish in the bell jar.

As soon as the researchers determined that the pike were reluctant to hurt themselves on this invisible barrier, they took the bell jar out of the aquarium and dumped all the minnows in with the pike. The result was that even though the glass barrier no longer protected the minnows, the pike made no attempt to eat them. The minnows could even swim right past the pike's noses and still the pike would not attack. The researchers concluded that if the experiment were to continue, the pike would eventually die from starvation, even with their food swimming around in front of them.

Let's face it, that's what has happened to a lot of us. We come into an organization with a lot of great ideas, lots of enthusiasm and spirit, and we get bonked on the nose. We end up thinking, "Well, if that's what it takes to survive around here, fine, I'll just show up and do my job."

An expression in the auto industry is, "Do my eight, hit the gate." This thinking happens to a lot of us. It inhibits growth, development, creativity, and all of those things that enable us to reach our full potential. We become rigid.

Yes, We Have No Bananas

Many experiments are done with monkeys, especially the Resis monkeys, as they more closely resemble the human animal. In one experiment, researchers placed a number of Resis monkeys into a room that had been specially designed. The monkeys were well fed, well looked after and well cared for. In this room there was a big hole in the ceiling, and an air conditioner that was rumbling away. Once a day, everyday, the researchers would lower a bunch of nice fresh bananas through the hole in the ceiling. However, when the monkeys would grab one of the bananas, their action would trip a switch that would activate the air conditioner. As a result, the monkeys would receive a blast of icy air. The shot of cold air would be so uncomfortable for them that it would cause them to release the banana and scatter away from the offered treat.

The next day, the same process would occur, and again the monkeys would scatter. Each day, the researchers repeated the scenario and the monkeys would run away from the cold blast…and the food. After a few days, when the bananas were lowered, the monkeys would not go near them. Very soon, none of the monkey subjects would approach their favorite food. Then the researchers turned off the air conditioner. After that, no matter how many times the researchers lowered the bananas into the room, the monkeys would not attempt to approach or grab any of the bananas.

The most interesting part of the experiment, however, is what happened next. After all the monkeys refused to approach the bananas, for fear of a cold blast of air, the researchers began to change the makeup of the group. Once a day, every day, they removed one monkey from the room and replaced it with a new monkey who had never experienced the cold blast of air. They continued to lower the bananas and, as they predicted, the monkeys who had experienced the cold blast of air continued to avoid the bananas.

But the strange part is that the newly introduced monkeys also avoided the lowered food. The researchers continued to replace the monkeys one by one, each day, until not one monkey in the room had ever experienced the cold blast of air. Then they lowered the bananas again. You have probably guessed it—none of the monkeys went to take a banana.

If you were to take one of those monkeys and ask, "Why don't you go and eat one of those bananas?" the monkey would probably look at you and say, "Well, that's just not the way it's done around here!"

Is that statement familiar at all? Have you ever heard someone you work with, or for that matter yourself, say, "You know we tried that back in 1982. If I recall correctly, someone tried to sue us or something because of it, so we don't do that anymore."

We see examples occurring in organizations where people are still using old practices, put in place many, many years ago. In some cases, the reason for the practice is no longer known. Nevertheless, these practices have become such an ingrained part of the culture, that every new person coming in picks them up and does not even question the rationale.

Sadly, we have seen managers today behave the same way their managers did 20 to 30 years ago—and sadly it didn't work that well back then. Even so, they continue to repeat the same behavior and it sure doesn't work any better today. Perhaps, then, we can't fault the researchers for assuming that we do, at times, behave like trained monkeys.

Strategies for Dealing with Change

We recognize that managers and employees alike find managing change to be a difficult task. To make the process easier we suggest the following strategies.

- **Acknowledge reactions.** *Everyone affected will have a reaction.* It is important to be aware of this. Even positive change is a transition; therefore, even those who will be pleased with the changes will have some reactions they did not expect.
- **Deal with emotions.** *Recognize and deal with emotions constructively.* It is important that everyone accepts their own feelings for what they are and channels them appropriately. Find a suitable and harmless means of expressing them. Share them with those you trust, write them down or even speak into a recorder.
- **Identify adjustments.** *Identify what adjustments people need to make.* You will be able to play a major role here for all people concerned. Individuals may require some guidance regarding changes they need to make and how they might approach the new organization and their role in it.
- **Understand phases.** *Understand the different phases of managing change.* Sharing this information with all the people who are affected will promote a greater degree of understanding among the whole group. The sharing will create a bond and a new language to use in discussing and making sense of what is happening to the people and the organization.
- **Manage stress.** *Manage the stress of traumatic change.* Instigate

some workshops or employ some change specialists to help everyone deal with the stress. Send the message that the organization acknowledges that everyone has felt the impact of traumatic change and is willing to do something about it. We also suggest you read the section entitled *Effective Communication Reduces Stress* in Chapter 5, Communication.

Four "C"s for Coping with Change

The work of researchers, including Cynthia Scott and Dennis Jaffe, has shown that some people cope with change better than others. Their research data and personal experience shows that people who can withstand the stress of change utilize certain key skills. These are not personality traits but actual skills that employees can learn. They have identified four key skills that are found in hardy, stress-resistant workers. We call them the four "C"s for coping with change.

- **Commitment**—They are involved in their work and they create a sense of purpose and meaning in what they do.
- **Control**—They experience a sense of personal power and look for what they can control in their jobs.
- **Challenge**—They see change as an opportunity to learn new skills, not as something they must avoid and fear.
- **Connection**—They value their friendships with people, feel respected, and have a common bond and purpose with the people around them.

Employees commanding these skills are better able to reduce the negative effects of change on their work performance, personal functioning and health.

The Power to Change

"That's just the way I am. I can't change it." Have you ever made that statement? If you have, you are deceiving yourself. We all can change our behavior, at any time, at any age. You, too, can change and begin to do the things you choose to make a healthy workplace.

The first step is to want to change. However, desire is not enough. You have to *believe* you can change.

Throughout history, there have been innumerable examples of ordinary people achieving the extraordinary. The one factor common to all of these successful people is that they believed they could do it. As authors, we do realize that you are not reading this book to change the world or to break any records. Most likely you just want to have a healthier workplace. Nevertheless, you still need to be aware of how your own thinking will determine your success or failure—and you need to apply the same principles as any other successful person.

Let's look at just one case of the incredible power of believing that you can achieve your goals.

The event happened on May 6, 1954. That was the day Roger Bannister ran the mile in 3 minutes, 59.4 seconds, and set a new world record. He became the first athlete in history to run a mile in less than four minutes—a record that medical and sport experts had said could *never* be broken.

While many had tried to break this barrier previously, no one had ever done it. The experts were suggesting the barrier was real, and that human beings were not capable of running any faster. Then along came Roger who believed it could be done.

Roger Bannister, who was knighted in 1975, was a British physician who had a passion for running. He believed he could prove the experts wrong. He trained very hard and kept practicing.

It's probably worth mentioning that for centuries other human beings had been doing the training and practicing as well, yet they never broke the four-minute barrier. They settled for the title of the fastest person on earth, during that year. They believed they had run as fast as any human could, until that day in 1954 when Roger proved them wrong.

The incredible thing about Bannister's achievement was that it changed the belief systems of other runners. Less than two months later, the Australian athlete, John Landy, also broke the four-minute mile, and set another record of 3 minutes 58 seconds. Later that year, Bannister defeated Landy in a mile race held in Vancouver, Canada. Even though neither set a new record, both Roger and John broke the four-minute barrier again. Today, you don't even qualify for a world-class event unless you run the mile in less then four minutes.

Sometimes we need another person to prove to us that something can be done. One person can help us change our thinking, and thereby, change our behavior. Countless numbers of people have made their workplace better. Think of them when you need inspiration. You, too, can make it happen and have the career or the work environment you desire. You can change yourself and be the kind of person you want to be. As many people have proven, your ability to create a healthy workplace depends greatly on your belief that you can. If you believe you can, you will. If you believe you can't, you won't.

Never underestimate the power of your own thinking.

Career

Align Your Profession with Your Passion

**The majority work to make a living; some work to
acquire wealth or fame, while a few work because
there is something within them which demands
expression....Only a few truly love it.**
Edmund Boreaux Szekely

Career Development in the New Millennium

Recruiting and keeping talented people is a major challenge facing organizations today. *Retention management* is a buzzword of the new millennium. In fact, keeping star performers has become a high priority.

One of the best ways to achieve employee retention is to create a synergy between the lives of the individuals and the mission of the organization. The key is to create a balance between the people and the business goals.

Increasingly, people are recognizing that strategic talent matching and career development are critical elements for retaining star performers.

Retention happens when people love what they do.

The healthiest workplaces consist of people doing what they love to do, and doing it in an environment that supports and encourages the development of their talents, skills and abilities.

Who's Responsible?

The responsibility for career development begins with the individual. In reality, many of us are driven to achieve some form of meaningful work. Our clients have confirmed this truth. In our discussions, they have said they believe the studies that reveal people in their later years are less afraid of dying than they are of not having made a contribution to society.

The process of developing a career and doing something meaningful can be a difficult one. Many seek out help with this process—most often looking to the workplace to find the answers and the support.

We believe the responsibility for career development is best assigned in the following manner:

1. **The individual provides the initiative**. It is up to each individual to discover their own unique talents and to take the responsibility for managing their careers.
2. **The manager provides the coaching.** An important skill for managers to acquire is the ability bring out the best in their people. They need to know about their peoples' aspirations and then provide the opportunity to let them do what they were meant to do.
3. **The organization provides the resources**. Investing in the process of strategic talent matching will have a positive effect on the bottom line. Failing to provide such a resource will simply lead to people looking to develop their career options elsewhere.

Who Wants to Work?

Let's face it. You spend a lot of your waking hours at work. In fact, you probably spend more than 2,000 hours a year working. And during those hours, how much time do you spend dreaming about, or looking forward to, some type of leisure activity? We're willing to bet that the answer involves a significant amount of time.

Looking forward to, and finding, some kind of leisure time is actually becoming a problem for many people. Remember those experts in the 1960s who predicted that with the continuing development of technology we would all have more free time in the future? They were even bold enough to say that the typical workweek would consist of only three days, leaving us four days to enjoy ourselves in some kind of leisure activity.

Clearly, they were wrong. Most of us today work even longer and harder then we did back in those wishful days. What used to be a typical 40-hour workweek has currently stretched, for many, to 45, 50 and even more hours. Sometimes, we are checking our e-mails and responding to work-related enquiries late at night and even on weekends.

Adding to the picture is the fact that there are more of us in the workforce. The current statistics show that employment in general is up by 10 percent. Self-employment represents one of the fastest-growing trends in today's workplace. Analysts are even saying that in North America we are close to full employment, leading many to suggest that there are jobs for almost anyone who wants to work.

The number of women working has also changed dramatically in the past few decades. When the authors started work in the 1960s, women represented only four percent of the workforce. Now, they account for at least 40 percent. Further adding to the workforce numbers is the fact that more young people are entering the workforce, and older people are making the decision to continue long after the traditional retirement years.

Leisure and Work

In his popular book, *It's Not About Time! Rediscovering Leisure in a Changing World,* author and educator Joe Pavelka explores the concept of work. "Are we working more because we want to, have to, or just because we can?" Pavelka explains that during the latter half of the 20th century "the concept of work evolved into that of a career. This meant a shift from work as exclusively negative toward work as linked to aspirations, with an assumption that at some level most of us want to work. Our expectations also evolved to the point where most of us now expect a fairly high level of satisfaction and self-expression at work. During the 1980s, this was often referred to as empowerment. We recognize and expect that work should be more than a paycheck and that work and leisure should not be opposites."

Discover the Passion

For years now, career experts have been talking about the importance of doing what you love when choosing a career. The key factor to a successful career is to not only enjoy your work, but to love what you do. When you love what you do, you will tap into your intrinsic and creative forces—and you will succeed.

You will also begin to experience a burning desire. You will become passionate about doing what you love and loving what you do. People who have discovered this passion tend to say, "I can't believe I'm getting paid to do this!" Work for them has become an enjoyable experience. They begin to "do the common thing uncommonly well."

You may ask, "How will I find this passion—this career that I love?" The answer lies in discovering what you were meant to do and embarking on the road to self-discovery. The undertaking requires that you get in touch with yourself, to get an inside view of your preferences and your desires. It also requires that you recognize what you naturally enjoy most, that you discover your passion. Not only do you need to know what you were meant to do, you must truly understand that your life has a purpose.

It is all about choosing the right direction, in accordance with what you truly want. It means taking the time to know yourself and to become internally driven. As Marsha Sinetar states in her inspirational book, *Do What You Love, The Money Will Follow*, "The very best way to relate to our work is to choose it."

Making the right choice, and choosing to act according to your values, will lead to greater insight. You will discover your strengths and weaknesses, likes and dislikes, motivating and demotivating factors, and your fears.

The key is to trust yourself. Believe in your own perceptions and have faith that they will point you in the right direction.

Your Inner Compass

We are all blessed with an *inner compass* that, if left alone, will point us in the right direction. However, like an actual compass that is affected by external forces such as radio signals, certain metals, even the earth itself, our inner compass can be pointing in the wrong direction, because of influences from the outside.

Unfortunately, we are easily influenced by people and circumstances, and forget sometimes who we really are and what is important to us. Family, friends and teachers are just a few of the people who may have prejudiced our career choices. These prejudices can control us and force us into a mold of conformity, diminishing any thought or action that might develop our individuality and creativity. In short, we lose our way.

Writer Shakti Gawain notes, "Every time you don't follow your inner guidance, you feel a loss of energy, loss of power, a sense of spiritual deadness."

If you are living your life according to other people's expectations or restrictions, it is time to break free. The first step involves you defining your identity and becoming self-aware, seeing yourself as you really are, and getting in touch with your inner self. Your greatest strength and direction will come from inside you, not from the outside world.

To discover your purpose and direction in life, you need only look inside. To gain this insight it is important that you are honest with yourself and, above all, have faith and trust in your inner compass.

Trusting is new behavior for many of us and, not surprisingly, many of us have difficulty looking inside. We are afraid of what we may find. Perhaps we are afraid to learn that we are living a very restricted life. We might not want to accept that we have been staying put, because we choose security over challenge. We have been following the herd. As a result, we have been stopping ourselves from using our full potential and experiencing inner joy. Instead, we tend to be experiencing regret about what might have been, settling merely for the mundane because it is safe and predictable.

Looking inside and trusting our inner compass may be difficult and, as a result, we may react with skepticism. We tend to want to stay with what's familiar and doubt that this inner exploration will lead to any real change.

As people experienced in this process, we strongly suggest that you keep an open mind. Explore, experiment and reflect. Talk to someone who has successfully made this inner journey.

Write your thoughts and feelings in a daily journal. Experiment with yoga and meditation or spend time in nature to clear your mind. Once you confront your fear of self-discovery and take the steps to discover your innermost self, you will learn that you really had nothing to fear all along. You will begin to recover your own sense of identity. The fact is you will recover not only your sense of self, but also your sense of safety, power, integrity, connection and faith.

Begin your journey. Know that as you deepen your awareness and discover your inner compass, you are on the path that will lead to you experiencing the true joy of doing what you were meant to do.

Robert Louis Stevenson once said, "To know what you prefer instead of humbly saying Amen to what the world tells you you ought to prefer, is to have kept your soul alive."

Do what you were meant to do and you will be passionate, and from this passion the answers will come.

A Childhood Dream

Most often, the discovery of what you were meant to do began to develop when you were a child. You would play, pretend and dream about the kind of activities that would make you most happy. As you joyfully played, you began to learn new skills. The skills could then be used as you entered the world of work. Unfortunately, your childhood dreams and aspirations can start to fade, as outside forces impinge on your belief systems and attitudes.

Events during Luke's own childhood provide a perfect example. He was eight years old when he experienced the event that was to have a profound effect on the rest of his life.

One fateful day in Belgium, where he grew up, his parents had enrolled him in a junior talent show. Feeling nervous, yet excited, he began his performance. He sang a popular song about relationships and love. You can imagine the audience's positive reaction to a very young boy behaving as if he understood the meaning to an adult experience. In fact, they thoroughly enjoyed his efforts and demonstrated their pleasure by awarding him first prize. To this day he can still recall how proud and excited he felt.

The positive experience led him to volunteer in school when the teacher would ask someone to make a presentation. He thoroughly enjoyed doing them.

However, three years later life changed, when he immigrated to Canada with his parents. Learning a new language and adapting to a different culture created new fears and insecurities for Luke. School was especially scary, particularly starting grade seven in the middle of the school year.

One day during class, the teacher was giving a lecture about farming. He raised his hand because he didn't know the meaning of the word "soil" she kept using. After he asked her to explain what it meant, she responded with a rather curt reprimand that he should know such a simple word, and if he didn't, he should look it up in the dictionary. The class laughed. He felt devastated. He never asked another question for the rest of the year, and failed the grade.

Throughout his remaining school years he developed a very negative attitude about his learning abilities; he also never gave another presentation in front of the class.

Recover Your Passion

Thankfully, years later, Luke was fortunate to receive the attention of a caring mentor who saw the smoldering passion that lay quenched beneath the surface. He encouraged Luke to seek the help of a career counselor and begin the struggle to recover his lost dream.

Luke eventually returned to school as an adult learner and began his journey to recover his passion. Like Joe, Luke is a member of the Canadian Association of Professional Speakers and the National Speakers Association, which enables him to enjoy the experiences of engaging an audience.

As Pablo Picasso once said: "Every child is an artist. The problem is how to remain an artist once he grows up."

As you can see, it's worth beginning to recover your passion, the passion you first experienced when you were young and lost as you became an adult. We truly believe that discovering and recovering your passion will lead directly to your calling. Begin the journey.

More great things have been accomplished by passion and instinct, than by logic and reason.

Passion, however, is not enough. To say that passion will overcome everything, would be unrealistic. That would be like saying that if you discovered you were passionate about golf you could play in the Masters tournaments. The fact is, it takes years of hard work, training and practice to develop the skills to play at that level. Having a strong desire and knowing you will enjoy, even love, your calling is just the beginning. It is, though, the right beginning.

Your Life Story

Life can only be understood backwards;
but it must be lived forward.
Soren Kierkegaard

Writing a brief autobiography is one of the exercises career experts across the board tend to suggest as part of the career evaluation and assessment process.

One such expert, Richard Nelson Bolles, author of the famous career-planning book *What Color Is Your Parachute?*, suggests that "the best *career-change* method ever devised is to go back to square one, and inventory all over again what gifts you have been given, and what knowledge you have acquired."

In other words, discover your future through examining your past. Writing the story of your life will help you to get to know yourself better and gain further insight into what is important to you. Knowing where you have been will help you determine where you want to go next, or at the very least, where you don't want to go again.

We suggest that you write about 20 to 30 pages detailing the events of your life. It is perfectly acceptable, and for some preferable, to write an outline simply highlighting the events. Pay particular attention to the events and the people who had the greatest impact on your life. Remember some of the choices you made, or did not make, because of circumstances or significant people who influenced you.

Start at the beginning, describing your early years, illustrating some of your desires and fantasies, progressing through to the present. It is important that you include where you've been and what you've done both in your career and personal life. Don't forget the failures, as well as the successes. In fact, this is one exercise where you really might learn more from your failures than your successes.

Above all, enjoy it. Let your thoughts and insights flow easily. Simply be open to whatever experiences come to your consciousness without editing or censoring. It is your life, your values, your likes and dislikes, your wants and needs. It is not about *shoulds* or what other people might think. Go ahead, write *your* story.

Jim's Story

One of our clients, Jim, was in the beginning stages of a career assessment with us. During the initial meetings, he stated adamantly that he never wanted to be an accountant again. He had been an accountant for a large fast-food employer that had just terminated his employment. He was very vocal about "not wanting to do work like that ever again."

Under the circumstances, his desire to explore a different career seemed quite normal. When asked about his dreams and aspirations or, as we sometimes put it, "What do you want to be when you grow up?" Jim expressed his interest in opening a rare bookstore. In the store, he said he would make available "unique and hard-to-find treasures." It was obvious that he was talking about something he would love to do. He also said that someday he would write a book, and that he was taking some courses at the local college to learn how. What better person, you may ask, to write a brief autobiography.

Some weeks later Jim handed in his assignment. It was 217 pages long. That's right, more than 200 pages. At least one thing was obvious: Jim loved to write. However, his "brief" autobiography created a bit of a puzzle.

From the very beginning, when Jim chose accounting as his career, he described some of the problems he solved and the results he achieved. Clearly, he was proud of these accomplishments. His life story was filled with examples of him helping others to solve problems of an accounting nature. Jim was also very active as a volunteer in his church and two social clubs, fulfilling the role as tax advisor and accountant. For someone who hated accounting, he sure did a lot of it for free.

Needless to say, it was important to revisit Jim's career choice of being an entrepreneurial bookstore owner. After reviewing the autobiography with Jim, we expressed our surprise at reading so many accounting success stories, which Jim seemed to thoroughly enjoy. Then, we posed the "what if" question. "What if you were to be an accountant in a publishing house, surrounded by people who love books?" His eyes opened wide, a smile appeared on his face, and he said; "now — that would be fun." It was a perfect example of all the puzzle pieces falling into place.

Jim's story illustrates wonderfully how the "Life Story" exercise can help to clarify your choices and aspirations. Even though he at first expressed a strong disinclination to continuing in his current career, the review of his autobiography revealed the true story. It was the environment (the fast-food industry) to which he could not relate, not the work.

Discovering Your Strengths

Think back to the time you decided what to do for a living, or even when you chose the job you are in today. Most likely, you made that choice based on one criteria—what you do well. You would have considered an ability, a competence, something you had learned to do as a result of studying and practicing. Many of us, in fact, have learned our jobs as a result of repetition and working hard to get better—simply because we needed to make a living.

Our society reinforces this kind of development. We are told that if we work hard and put our minds to it, we will be successful. Our educational system further supports this process. It is designed to evaluate and assess what we're good at. We learn and we study, and at the end exams test our knowledge. The areas in which we receive the highest marks are considered to be our best subjects.

Low marks on the other hand often receive more attention, and usually the result is advice to work and study harder. After long hours of sweat and tears, we improve our grades and eventually graduate. After all, we are told failure is not an option.

Based on these results you may have been told to pursue certain careers. For example, if you are good with numbers you might choose accounting, while good chemistry results might influence you to look at research.

The pressure to choose based on your abilities, and to work hard to develop these abilities, can be further exacerbated by the influence of your parents who want to be proud of you. They might pressure you to pursue studies in areas where they feel you would be successful. Or they might have encouraged you to pursue a career in an area where *they* would be proud of you. They might have pushed you toward a profession highly valued for its money or status, such as a doctor or lawyer. Or they might have suggested that you go after that master's degree in business administration, just like your brother did.

To help you sort out your opinions on your abilities and your work, we have devised some graphs.

Using the following charts, rate yourself on your abilities.

Are You Able?

On the scale of 0 to 10, evaluate yourself honestly on how good you are at what you do.

Do You Enjoy Your Work?

Fun and enjoyment are highly underrated in most areas of our lives and that includes choosing our careers. The fact is that basing your career choice solely on your abilities is not enough. You need to include one other major factor, and that is: *What do you enjoy? What's fun for you?*

Most likely, when being given career advice on what type of job would be best, you were never asked, "What do you like to do?" The reality is that few of us were ever asked to consider the enjoyment factor as part of the career equation. Unfortunately, this approach has resulted in too many people doing jobs that they may be good at, but that they don't enjoy. As a result, they can't wait for the workday or week to end so they can go and do something enjoyable. In fact, they will often justify their hard work by saying that they are doing it to make the money to spend on something that is fun.

The answer to the dilemma, and the key to discovering your strengths, lies in discovering the right combination of enjoyment and abilities. Matching what you do best with what you enjoy will lead to your ideal position.

You will discover that your abilities to perform your job will continue to improve. Simply stated, if you are soaring with your strengths you will be enjoying your work. When we enjoy what we do, we are motivated to continue learning and improving.

Refer to the graph below and complete it.

Are You Doing What You're Meant to Do?

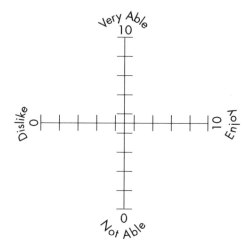

On a scale of 0 to 10, rate both your ability level and your level of enjoyment. Then draw a line connecting the two.

The Result

Where did your results fall? Did you fall on the *right* side of the graph, or the *left*? If you scored yourself high in both ability and enjoyment, we congratulate you. You are pursuing the right career. You are likely passionate about what you do and are willing to work hard to achieve your goals. You are also in the minority.

Our experience has shown that most people are on the *left* side. They may be good, or even very good, at what they do but they don't seem to enjoy themselves or find the job satisfying. Some are actually envied in their success, by their peers and associates, yet they are suffering from stress and may be relying on some type of controlled substance in order to help them continue in a job that gives them no satisfaction.

We have even met some individuals who are not very good at what they do *and* they hate it. You may have met some of these people. You will recognize them from the fact that they seem miserable and highly agitated.

If you scored yourself low in ability and high in enjoyment then that is also good. You are on the *right* side. You will discover that you are on the road to developing your talent.

Imagine what work would be like if you were able to simply do what you do best and what you love to do.

The Difference Between a Skill and a Talent

When asked the difference between a skill and a talent, you might respond by saying, "A talent is something that we are born with. It is innate, an inner strength that is a part of us. On the other hand, a skill is something we have learned."

Using that definition, we suggest that talents can be identified as a unique combination of something that motivates you and is enjoyable, and what you do best. Therefore, if you found yourself on the right side of the scale, you are working with your talents. If you were on the left side, you are using only your skills.

Let's use the analogy of learning to play a tune on the piano. Imagine a young child whose parents have purchased a piano. They are encouraging him to practice daily so that he will become proficient at playing the instrument. They even hire a music instructor to help their child become proficient. However, after many frustrating hours of demonstrating and teaching, the instructor proclaims that the child is tone deaf. Regardless, wanting to please his parents, the child perseveres and works hard. Eventually, by learning how to read music notes and memorizing where the right keys are, he develops the ability to play a tune. If he continued to work this hard, he would eventually develop the skill to play the piano.

Just like our young piano player, many people have learned the skills they use in their jobs. They have learned the information and practiced long and hard to improve. They have acquired jobs by memorizing "where the keys are." Yet, they still find it a struggle.

If, on the other hand, our young piano player had been born with a talent for music, learning to play the piano would have come easier. He would also find that he was motivated to play and practice. The work would be enjoyable. He might also discover that he could play other musical instruments, or be drawn to one instrument in particular. He would have what we call transferable skills.

The big advantage of working with your talents, particularly in today's fast-changing workplace, is that you will have transferable skills. You will be able to more easily adapt and remain employed.

It is our firm belief that if you are doing what you were meant to do, you will always make a living.

Another Piece of the Puzzle

A friend and associate of ours, known as Digger, believed he knew what he wanted to do from the time he was very young. He wanted to fly. Whenever an airplane would pass overhead he would look up and wish he were in the cockpit. All the money he made selling pop bottles and delivering groceries was spent on books about flight, flying and aircraft. The thought of flying an aircraft became his dream. Eventually, he acquired his pilot's license.

Digger applied to the airforce and the navy to become a pilot, and to military college to further his education. He was accepted to all three and a dilemma ensued. As he valued education first, he accepted the offer to attend military college, but...in the army!

One year after graduation, Digger faced another dilemma. His commanding officer told him he had been selected for army pilot training, at exactly the same time he was to be transferred to Europe. Digger selected pilot training over going to Europe and achieved his dream.

When he graduated from pilot training and received his wings, his problems began. Even though he spent long hours at the controls of a variety of airplanes, he was not happy.

One day, he asked a psychologist friend for some advice. He wanted to know why, after finally achieving his dream of being a pilot, he was beginning to dislike this longed-for career. His friend asked Digger to complete some assessment tools. After reviewing the results, he exclaimed, "No wonder you dislike being a pilot. You are an extreme, 'off-the-wall extrovert.' Sitting in the cockpit all by yourself for long periods of time without being able to interact with people would be painful."

The solution was contained in the fact that Digger liked to fly, but he liked to be with people more. Clearly the solitary activity of being a pilot was not for him.

What About the Weaknesses?

Up until now, we have presented mostly positive behaviors and preferences, but it is also important for you to identify your weaknesses. It is a generally accepted maxim that weaknesses are simply strengths that have been taken to an extreme. The crossover can often happen when you are under pressure and feeling anxious. Under these conditions you might lack confidence and use more of your strengths than are necessary, believing that more of a good thing will result in an even better performance. Unfortunately, when you overemphasize your strengths, they have a tendency to flip to the weakness side.

In case you find it difficult to believe, we've provided some common examples.

- You may be strong-willed, determined—good at directing and deciding. However, under pressure you may become autocratic. Or you may lose your temper and explode over what seems trivial.

If you are this type of person, you would benefit from pacing yourself, and knowing when and how to relax.

- You may be very friendly, compassionate, enthusiastic, and good at promoting and persuading. Under pressure you may oversell and manipulate. Also, since you are a "people person" and want to be liked, you struggle not to ever disappoint anyone.

If you are this type of person, you would benefit from understanding how, and when, to be more firm and direct in dealing with less-favorable situations.

- You may be very patient, loyal and predictable. You may also be steady and agreeable. Under pressure, you may give in, despite your needs. You may also become very uncomfortable with new situations and environments.

If you are this type of person, you would benefit from learning how to handle the reality of unexpected and ongoing change in a better way.

- You may pride yourself on being accurate and systematic. You love details and are very analytical, capable of taking a situation and breaking it down into each individual component. Under pressure, you may become perfectionistic and suffer from "analysis paralysis," the fear of making a decision because you believe you don't have all the details.

If you are this type of person, you would benefit from learning to develop a greater tolerance for conflict and human imperfection, including realistic approaches to preventing and minimizing both.

The Comfort Zone

As you can see from the above examples, whenever you are out of your comfort zone you run the danger of flipping to your weakness side. You could begin to overuse your strengths and apply "too much of a good thing" to the situation. The answer lies in accepting yourself as you are, and being in harmony with your internal feelings and preferences. When you stay focused on balancing your strengths according to what the situation demands, you will regain your confidence and feel in control.

The best part is that when you are being yourself, you will experience a flow of behavior that seems to happen without conscious thought. In the sporting world, this experience is often referred to as "zoning" or "flow." It is as if you are watching yourself perform. Your performance flows smoothly, without conscious effort and without trying. You are in "the zone." **You are experiencing joy.**

Providing the Resources

Career assessment tools are one of the powerful ways an organization can facilitate the process of strategic talent matching. Research evidence supports the conclusion that the most satisfied and productive individuals are those who know themselves, recognize the demands of the situation, and adapt strategies to meet those needs. These individuals are also able to explore workplace opportunities and choose their career according to their own unique personality type.

Over the years we have had the opportunity to complete and administer a variety of assessment tools. Properly applied and interpreted, these assessment tools will help you to understand yourself. These instruments can tell you about your strengths and weaknesses, your personality type, your preferences and the sorts of work that would best suit you.

Examples of these instruments will be described in later chapters. These instruments are available by contacting the authors directly by e-mail at: luke@thecouplescoach.com or joe@ethos.on.ca.

How to Use the Results

Career assessment tools can provide a plan to help you better understand yourself. While using them will help you see matters from your own perspective, you may still find it more difficult to see things from another person's viewpoint. Since both perspectives are necessary, seeing both is a challenge that is well worth the effort. By being able to see things differently, to be aware of a variety of points of view, you will be open to a greater number of possibilities and opportunities. You will increase your ability to find the right fit.

A Word of Caution About Assessment Tools

We do have a word of warning. No assessment tool is comprehensive enough, nor capable of capturing the full richness of a person. The full range of emotions, desires, thoughts and potential can only be described by the individuals themselves. Yet, we have seen people confuse an assessment model with the person. Some people will identify themselves as a certain type, as if they are always and forever fixed. They ignore the fact that these assessment tools are only meant to reveal tendencies and preferences, and that the outcome can and will be influenced by the individual and the outside world. They lose sight of their own uniqueness and their potential to change.

James Flaherty, author of the insightful book *Coaching: Evoking Excellence in Others*, writes, "Remember that human beings in every case will exist beyond the borders of whatever model is used to describe them; that a model is at best a well-focused snapshot; and that human beings are living, changing, adapting, and self-interpreting."

There is a danger that assessment tools can lead to a self-fulfilling prophecy. If a person accepts the instrument to be an inflexible assessment of who they are, what they prefer and how they behave, they may accept this label and only see themselves within the narrow confines of the assessment model. We all know the hazard of being labeled by someone. The power of a teacher on young person's life has been well documented. If a teacher believes a child is a low performer and treats that child according to that label, the child will often come to believe that he or she is a low performer and behave accordingly—though they may be very bright.

How often have you labeled yourself? Affixing labels to your forehead that say, "I'm not smart enough," "I'm just a shy person," "I don't have the talent to do that," limit your possibilities. **Beware of the power of labels.**

Consequently, we do suggest that you use these career assessment tools in the spirit for which they were designed. They are designed to help increase your awareness and gain a better understanding of your unique preferences, likes and dislikes. As such, they certainly help you to achieve career satisfaction if they are employed only as another tool to aid in the exploration of what you are meant to do.

The key to a successful career lies in discovering what you enjoy doing most, and to begin doing it.

De Sadeleer's "Career Magic"©

"Is there a formula that can help me to do what I *really* want to do for the rest of my life?"

In answer to that request Luke has spent some years developing a model that has become known as the *"Career Magic"©* success formula. We present it here in the hope that it will provide you with another way to consciously choose what you were meant to do. **We hope it will help you align your profession with your passion.**

The model incorporates the acronym **MAGIC**. Each letter represents an important factor for success.

M—motivation

In order to achieve what you want, you have to be willing to invest the necessary effort to make it happen. You are the only one who can motivate yourself to do the hard work necessary to achieve success. As someone once said, **"Success comes before work only in the dictionary."**

A—attitude

You need to believe in yourself. People who believe in themselves, who have a positive mental attitude, have many advantages when it comes to choosing the right career. These confident people are able to pay attention to their inner voice and choose one career over another. As Zig Ziglar, one of the world's best-known sales professionals and motivational speakers, once said, **"When we change the input into our minds, we change the output into our lives."**

G—goals

"If you don't know where you are going, how can you expect to get there?" Basil Walsh asked this pertinent question.

You need a focus, a direction to achieve success. You also need to have SMART goals. They are: Specific, Measurable, Attainable, Relevant and Time-bound.

Another important factor is your ability to anticipate the rewards inherent in reaching your goals. **The more clearly you can visualize the rewards for reaching your goal, the greater is its motivational pull.**

I—insight

Insight is the *magic wand* that will create the spark to light up your journey. The secret to discovering career satisfaction is to get in touch with yourself first. You need to focus internally before focusing externally on what you will need to do to make it happen. If you take the time to know yourself, you become internally driven.

Embark on the road to self-discovery, and you will come to understand that your life has a purpose. **Believe in the power of your inner compass to guide you in the right direction.**

C—commitment

How many promises have you made that you didn't keep? If your answer is "a few," then you need to know that one of the best ways to increase your chances of keeping your commitments and meeting your goals is to write out a self-contract. Write down what you are willing to do to achieve the career of your dreams. Then, sign your self-contract and date it.

Another important step to keeping your commitments is to let another person know what you want to achieve. Find a career mentor and share what you plan to do to put your career on the right track. It is also helpful to occasionally review your contract with them.

Finally, remember that people make decisions with their head, and make commitments with their heart. **The most powerful commitment is one that makes sense in your head and feels right in your heart.**

What Is Your Career Satisfaction IQ?

The first step to improving career satisfaction is to determine how satisfied you are currently. You need to have a measurement of your level of satisfaction, before you can develop a strategy on how and what to improve. After reading each question, give yourself a score of one to five. When you finish, add up your score and review the results.

Never		Sometimes		Always
1	2	3	4	5

1. Are you doing what you do best and enjoy? _____
2. Do you believe your work is meaningful and important to you? _____
3. Do you have a career goal and a focus? _____
4. Do you know what environment enables you to do your best work? _____
5. Are you taking responsibility for enhancing your career? _____
6. When you are fully engaged in your work, do you feel energized? _____
7. Can you articulate with passion your interests and abilities to others? _____
8. Do you seek guidance from others who are successful in your chosen career? _____
9. Do you continually work at improving and expanding your skills? _____
10. Are your values in sync with what you do for a living? _____
11. Do you feel confident and secure in the way you work with others? _____
12. Do you trust your inner compass to guide you? _____

Enter your total points here: _____

Results

40 or above: Congratulations. You are experiencing career satisfaction. Continue to take responsibility for improving your career and pursuing your passion. Choosing to do the work you enjoy will improve your emotional and physical health.

Below 40: Review what career choices you have made. Determine what changes you could make and what actions you will take to improve your career satisfaction. Trust your inner compass to guide you to the work you were meant to do.

Add your own: There may be other important factors to determine your career satisfaction that are not described in this exercise. Feel free to list these factors below. Score these factors and add the points to your results.

Additional factors that contribute to your career satisfaction:

_____

_____

_____

_____

_____

_____

Culture

Shared Values and Fundamental Beliefs

**Who you are and how you will be remembered,
is the sum of the value you contribute to society
and the values by which you live.**

The Importance of Values

To consider values in the workplace is to probe the very reason people work and why they behave in the ways they do, in their jobs. Values give meaning to life and work and provide fulfillment.

Values represent your most basic fundamental beliefs. They are the principles that will arouse an emotional reaction, if you perceive them to be threatened. They can also spur on your greatest achievements. If your work incorporates your values, you are likely to find that what you do is meaningful, purposeful and important. Anne Greenblatt, from Stanford University, states it very well when she says, "When your work is aligned with your values, you tap into the 'fire within.' The highest achievements of people and organizations arise when people feel inspired to accomplish something that fits their top values."

Let's face it, you spend more time at work than in any other single activity, including sleeping. It is therefore crucial that the place where you work, a place that has the greatest potential to satisfy your basic needs, has a code of conduct that easily matches your primary values.

Bottom line, if the people you work with don't respect your values, you'll find another place to work. Conversely, if you don't respect or honor your organization's values, you will be asked to leave.

Aligning the employees' values with the organizational values is a critical element in retention management.

Trucks Are Our Number One Resource

In our work as trainers and management consultants, we meet with many corporations. Before these meetings one of the first things we attempt to do is to assess whether the corporation truly values its people. This assessment process typically starts when we enter the foyer of the building. We look around and frequently find framed posters of the organization's *vision* or *mission statement* that quite regularly contains a statement that says, "People are our number one resource."

We tell corporate leaders, "That's great! People should be your number one resource." Then we ask, "How often do you enroll your people in personal development programs, or let them get together at a conference so they can learn from each other and share experiences?" Unfortunately, some of them say, "We don't have time for that," or "It's not in the budget this year."

Then we point to vehicles in the parking lot, with the company name on the side, and ask, "Do you ever take your company trucks in for maintenance?" They usually reply, indignantly: "Certainly! We always ensure they are running efficiently, and safely." Our response is, "In that case, you should change your statement to "Trucks are our number one resource."

It seems that some organizations put more effort and money into looking after their vehicles, than they do their people.

Is an Organization's Culture Important?

Thomas Hobbes, who lived in the 16th century, imagined a world without morality. He concluded that the result would be simple. There would be no farming, because others would help themselves to the farmer's labor. There would be no building, because others would move in and throw the builder out. There would be no art, because everyone would be concerned about their own basic survival.

There wouldn't be a calendar, because no one would adhere to it. Promises would be meaningless, because no value would be placed on keeping one's word. People would kill each other whenever it proved advantageous. Life would be, in Hobbes' words, "solitary, poor, nasty, brutish and short."

What saves us from this type of world is our ability to create a moral code by which we all agree to live. Hobbes called it a "social contract." The basic premise is I will respect you and yours, and you respect me and mine. It is an enlightened premise, but a difficult one to enforce.

What's to stop someone from breaking the agreement and taking advantage of the situation? Laws and punishments have some effect, but the law cannot cover every situation and catch every violator. There has to be something more to hold the contract together.

Hobbes recognized that in order to exist as a society, we require a general, built-in desire to live cooperatively, in order for us to keep promises for the sake of keeping promises and abstain from violence because violence is undesirable in and of itself. Adherence to a basic moral code needs to be as natural as breathing air, if we are to create a life that is communal, rich, kind, generous and lengthy.

Similarly, removing obstacles within the workplace, especially fear, is key to building a new culture. New leaders must be culture builders, providing direction and purpose. They must also encourage it by example. We have heard that if you want to determine the culture of an organization, look at their last ten promotions to senior management. The characteristics of these people say it all.

Developing Values

There are important elements to remember when establishing values. Organizations must consider the two or three fundamental beliefs that are critical to their success, when they are translated into behaviors. Many times they are a reflection of past reputation and the behavioral code of conduct within the organization.

Once values are established, they should be clearly articulated and understood by all employees. There should also be consequences in the form of reinforcement for appropriate behaviors and decisions that encourage these principles. Staff should also know, up front, that any conduct in violation of this code could result in disciplinary action or dismissal—even if there was a business benefit, which resulted in increased profit or revenue.

While organizational values provide the framework within which employees must work, personal values provide the framework from which employees approach their work. They represent a person's character—who he or she really is. In order for people to be happy and successful in their careers, both sets of values need to be understood and acknowledged. If a person finds they are working in an organization whose business conduct is not in alignment with their own personal values, that person will never find happiness and true success in that organization.

For an organization to be successful it must position values as the foundation on which its vision, mission and strategic objectives are created. As Ken Blanchard and Sheldon Bowles state in their inspiring book, *Gung Ho!*, "In a gung-ho organization values are the real boss. Values are to guide your behavior—you have to ensure the organization is internally aligned—everyone singing from the same hymn book."

Most successful organizations have two, three and maybe even four values which must be articulated and defined in terms of behaviors. Then the organization must go through the process of ensuring that all employees "buy in" to these values.

The biggest problem with achieving employees' buy-in is credibility. They may see the values as a poster on the wall, but if they do not observe executives modeling them appropriately, reinforcing them on a day-to-day basis and being consistent with how violation is handled, the values will remain just that—posters on the wall.

How all managers behave must be a reflection of the culture now desired by the organization.

You are about to determine your critical values. The good news is there is plenty of choice. The bad news is, you cannot have them all. A 'values exercise' can be found on the following pages. Review those values listed and answer the questions that follow.

Values Exercise

Below is a list of values. Please refer to the questions on the following pages.

Value	Attributes	Ranking
Accomplishment	completes tasks and gets results	_____
Acknowledgment	to be appreciated and rewarded	_____
Ambitious	hard-working, aspiring	_____
Broad-minded	open-minded	_____
Capable	competent	_____
Challenge	active and excited	_____
Cheerful	lighthearted, joyful	_____
Consistent	predictable	_____
Cooperation	getting along with others	_____
Courageous	stand up for beliefs	_____
Creative	lateral thinker	_____
Daring	risk-taker	_____
Dependable	keeps word	_____
Disciplined	follows orders	_____
Effective	efficient	_____
Expertise	being an expert in specific area	_____
Fair	even-handed	_____
Fastidious	fussy, detailed	_____
Forgiving	willing to pardon	_____
Friendship	to have valuable friends	_____
Helpful	works for others' welfare	_____
Honest	sincere, truthful	_____
Imaginative	dreamer	_____
Independent	self-reliant	_____
Instructive	shares information with others	_____
Intimacy	shares deep affection	_____

Loving	tender, affectionate	_____
Open	accepting	_____
Organization	logical, consistent, rational	_____
Pleasure	contentment, pleasure, fun	_____
Polite	well-mannered	_____
Quality	high standards	_____
Recognition	awards, status, well-known	_____
Responsible	reliable	_____
Security	protection, safety	_____
Spiritual	inner peace	_____
Self-controlled	restrained	_____
Tranquil	peace, quiet, no conflict	_____
Variety	enjoys new experiences	_____
Wealth	financial independence	_____

Refer to the values list on the previous page and rank the top five in the order you believe are most encouraged by your organization:

1. _____
2. _____
3. _____
4. _____
5. _____

How have you seen these demonstrated in your organization the past 12 months?

_____

_____

_____

_____

_____

Now go back to the same list and rank the top five in the order you believe best represents your most strongly held personal beliefs:

1. _____
2. _____
3. _____
4. _____
5. _____

Do any appear on both lists? Were there any on one list that were in conflict to those on the other list? Can the differences be resolved?

We find that in order for people to be truly successful in their profession, there should be synergy between the two lists.

Phases of Organizational Development

Just like people, organizations go through a number of predictable phases before establishing an operating culture, or code of behavior. Let's review these phases.

In the beginning, all organizations are formed because a person, or a group of people, has a dream. The dream could be about a product they would like to bring to market, a service they want to provide to industry or a benefit they want to bestow upon a community. The initial stage is what we call the *entrepreneurial phase*.

Entrepreneurial Phase

During the entrepreneurial phase, people work together without the benefit of an organizational chart or policy manual. It tends to be a high-energy workplace and, because of that, a fun place to work. Those involved all understand the reputation they want to have in the industry and abide by a set of values, even though those values usually are not articulated. In this organization, everyone communicates with each other.

For instance, the shipping room clerk may be struggling with one of his work challenges. If the president walks by, the two people might engage in a discussion on how the packages should be bundled. Or, in another part of the firm, a sales person might go to the boss and say, "I think I have a prospect out in Vancouver." The boss might reply, "Good luck. Do you need some cash or a credit card? You know what is best, do whatever it takes."

Over the long term, however, if a company continues working in this manner, it will be following a going-out-of-business strategy. A firm's founder will soon realize they must institute some controls and processes. The realization will take them into the *bureaucratic phase*.

Bureaucratic Phase

During the bureaucratic phase, they develop an organizational chart. Sometimes this chart is a mile wide and a mile deep. Some organizations have been known to create as many as 16 levels of management. If you really think about it, there are only two people in any organization who are really valued, the one who decides what to do and the other who does it, everyone else is overhead. Perhaps this is a stretch, but 16 is certainly too many levels.

In our experience, the optimum number of management levels is five, whatever the size of the organization. If you look at some of the most efficient companies or organizations, even the religious ones, they are usually set up in such a way. Fortunately, companies soon come to realize that too much bureaucracy is stifling to creativity and productivity. It just takes too long to make decisions. In addition, the people making the critical decisions are many levels removed from the customer—and the organization loses touch.

Silos Phase

To fix the ratio of management to employees, many companies have gone through massive downsizing and restructuring. Many of the people displaced were middle managers. At the same time, other companies started breaking up into smaller entrepreneurial organizations, creating specific lines of business (LOB's), strategic business units (SBU's) or other divisions, focused on specific products or services. We call this phase the *silos phase*. Elliott Jaques details the benefits of this phase in his book *Requisite Organization*.

Although the transition will have fixed the issue of customer focus, a few problems could arise from this phase. The heads of each of these new business units or divisions could become engaged in what we call "empire building," with each unit vying for its own human resources department, research and development function and sales force. If these desires are satisfied, the result is redundancy—duplication of effort and additional costs not supported by higher revenue. During this phase it can also happen that none of the silos will communicate with each other. The lack of communication causes frustration on the part of the employees. The other negative situation that could arise is that employees may scatter their energies, chasing ideas designed only for short-term gain. These efforts may divert them from the company's core business strengths—often with disastrous results.

As we are discovering, in developing through the different phases, organizations experience a different set of problems at each stage. What we see especially during the silos phase, is that companies are organized like a pack of hungry wolves. Departments, functions and business units fight with each other for budgets, resources, promotions and customer face time.

In short, units do not collaborate with each other. Instead, they compete. Employees notice and believe that this is indicative of the basic culture of the company. Customers get calls from sales people from the various units seeking their business. Confused and frustrated, they develop preferred supplier contracts. Finally, since the purchasing process is a time-consuming and expensive one, they look for other less troublesome alternatives.

In the event that the firm has chosen to deal with inquiries by contracting out the first-line contact with customers, other less-than-favorable results can occur. Customers who do call may have their call transferred to a telemarketing group working in another province, state or even country—and the people answering the phone may be less than polite or lacking in knowledge. Eventually, these customers leave in search of a company that really wants their business.

Matrix Phase

To remedy these issues, organizations will usually go to the next phase we call the *matrix phase*. It is still a form of silo, but the focus has shifted from products or services to customers or geographic coverage. Consequently, there is only one HR manager across all functions or divisions, one R & D manager, and one account manager. While the matrix phase fixed many of the problems encountered with the silos phase, it also created new ones. The most significant of these is an exponential increase in the number of "meetings." People become difficult to contact because they are always in meetings.

Some companies have even gone so far as to come up with new names for meetings in order to disguise them. They call them networking sessions, interlocking events, cross-functional synergy sessions or dialogue opportunities. You get the idea. They might even have meetings to decide when to have future meetings. Under any name they are still meetings, and employees come to hate them. Many of them are unproductive and add no value to making effective decisions, getting things done or keeping customers happy.

At this point, a number of forward-thinking organizations have begun to ask, "Is there a better way?" Certainly there is value to having an efficient bureaucracy, there is value to having silos focused on customers, and there is value to cross-functional synergies that work across the organization, instead of in separate silos.

Structure is necessary, but wouldn't it be nice if we could also capture the spirit and enthusiasm displayed by employees during the entrepreneurial phase?

Empowered Teams

What these forward-thinking companies did was dissect the elements that could make it work. One of the basic elements that came out was values. During the entrepreneurial phase, this was the guide people used to make their decisions. For example, they knew their reputation was the most important aspect of long-term success. Another element was for all the people in the firm to share the same dream. Since, in the 1990s, it was not good to be heard talking about your dreams in corporations, they came up with the word 'vision'. In its simplest form, vision is the dream for which the corporation is striving. It is the guiding light on the other side of the ocean, which we hope to reach.

As well, during those early stages, everyone knew why they came to work, and the consequences of accomplishing (or not) what they had to do. This knowledge became their mission—the reason they came to work on a day-to-day basis. Each organization should be able to answer one fundamental question: What is the reason for your organization's existence today? The one-sentence answer to this would become the organization's mission statement.

Out of the values-vision-mission framework, organizations then create their strategic objectives. These objectives are annual goals that should be focused on the three key areas to ensure success for the organization. The key areas are as follows.

1. **Business requirements.** This area is measured by such items as revenue growth, profit, market share, return on investment,

return on assets, earnings before income tax, depreciation and amortization, and return on total assets. Most organizations are good at planning and tracking these on a monthly, quarterly or annual basis.

2. **Customer satisfaction.** This important area has loyalty measures such as repeat business, satisfaction surveys and complaint letters. Our studies show that less than 50 percent of organizations are taking a proactive approach and tracking these with a strategy for improvement on a regular basis.

3. **Employee satisfaction.** This area is also measured in terms of loyalty, but also by attrition, punctuality, morale assessment surveys, and executive interviews. We find that less than 20 percent of Canadian organizations have a strategy and measurement system to take care of this area.

These three fundamental areas should always be kept in balance. If one does very well to the detriment of the others, it will ultimately damage the organization.

When an organization completes the whole process, it is then able to go on to the next phase, which is *empowered teams*. This is when all employees, managers, associates and union members connect. They connect because they have now all bought into, will benefit from, and are committed to the organization's strategic plan.

Making "Right" Choices

To really empower teams, companies need to ensure that they are able to make the 'right' decisions—right for the customer, right for the employee and right for the business. There are two steps to this process.

The first is developing a "go-no-go" model for value-based decisions. Remember, we do not want to create a bunch of bureaucratic rules. After the team decides the course of action it wants to take, it gathers all the relevant information around that decision. Who are the stakeholders? Who has any issues? What will their issues be? After they have gathered all the facts, they must then determine if the course of action is appropriate according to three ethical criteria:

1. **Utility.** Does the decision optimize the satisfaction of everyone involved?
2. **Rights.** Does it respect the rights of individuals involved?
3. **Justice.** Is it consistent with the cannons of justice?

If the answer is clearly "no" on all three criteria, then the team should come to a full stop. If it is clearly "yes" on all three criteria, then the team may proceed without requiring higher approval.

However, the tough decisions are those that are "no" on just one or two criteria, and in which it would be a great benefit to the organization to proceed. At this point the team will have to do a more in-depth analysis and explore questions such as the following:

1. Are there any overwhelming factors, which should be considered, that will weigh it in one direction or another?
2. Is one criterion more important than the others in this situation?
3. Are there any incapacitating factors?

Once the teams have delved into these issues, the next step is to determine the risk of something going wrong. The groups will look at risk from two sides, or what we call a *two-dimensional axis*:

1. What is the **probability** of error?
2. What is the **consequence** of the error?

At this stage, these steps involve analyzing the probability of error. Is it high or is it low? They will do the same for the consequence. Is it high or low? If it is low on both dimensions, then the team should proceed with caution. If it is high on both, the course of action should not be considered.

If they fall in the median range, the team then should do a risk-mitigation analysis to see what could be done to either lower the probability or lower the consequence, or both. If this is achieved, then again, the team can proceed with caution with perhaps adi-tional sign-off from senior management.

Why do we put this decision-making process in this section for teams? In our experience, the above process is what great executives do. Interestingly enough, many of them do not even realize this is the subconscious thought process they go through. If teams do this, it will help develop the executive decision-making skills of its members and ensure there will be no violation of the culture or the strategic plan.

Live the Vision

An organization's vision represents the dream they would like to achieve. If achieved, there may no longer be a need for the organization to exist in its current form. The vision is the beacon of light keeping the entire organization focused on the course to being a world-class provider of its particular products or services.

Understanding the vision, however, is not enough. Leaders today must be able to inspire others towards it. This kind of inspiration not only involves their headspace, but their *heartspace* as well. It's impor-tant that employees have enthusiasm towards their profession and like doing work they feel will matter. A vision-driven organization recognizes that people want to succeed and want the organization to succeed.

A survey done by *Psychology Today* magazine indicated that more than 90 percent of workers surveyed said they want to produce the highest-quality work possible. In that same survey, however, more than 50 percent said they only work hard enough to keep their jobs. The reason they gave was that they were frustrated with management practices and top-down policies.

In order to tap into true employee enthusiasm, leaders must give people authority to make decisions about their work, tear down the old top-down, authority-based cultures, and inspire them to invest in the renewed future of the organization.

A story we heard years ago exemplifies the ideal perfectly. While a well-known leader in quality was consulting at the NASA organization, he found that everyone was happy and enthusiastic about their jobs, even the janitorial staff. Fascinated, he approached one gentleman and asked, "Why are you are so happy coming to work every day?" The janitor replied that it was because he had such an important job. To which the consultant said, "You are a janitor, you sweep floors and empty waste baskets." "No," the janitor replied. "I am part of the team that is going to put a man on the moon."

Clearly, NASA had captured the power of having a vision, which it had properly articulated and communicated throughout the organization. A well-articulated vision statement will result in new and invigorated working relationships and employee loyalties.

Do the employees in your organization know the true vision of the organization?

Purpose is the most powerful motivator in the world.
Ghandi

Now the Mission

The *mission statement* of an organization should answer the basic question, "What is the reason for our existence right now?" It should be only one sentence and articulate clearly the following items:

- Who are we?
- What is it we do?
- For whom do we do it?
- Why do we do it?

However, simply stating the mission is not enough. It must be exciting, memorable, and inspire commitment. It must be customer-focused, be written in a way that makes employees proud, and gives them a reason to be excited to come to work. It must go beyond the focus of revenue or profit.

In our seminars we ask participants if they know the mission statements of highly successful organizations. They invariably answer "yes" and, surprisingly, many can state them. We then ask, "Does your organization have one?" About 50 percent raise their hands. We then ask, "Who here can state theirs right now?" Only about five percent are able to do this without referring to some material.

Can all employees in your organization articulate the mission without reading it?

Goals and Objectives

Every organization must develop objectives on an annual basis based on business and industry requirements. The goals must be well balanced among profit goals, customer goals and employee goals. There should also be a target for each area which management is inspired to achieve.

As we stated previously, if one is achieved at the expense of another, there will be long-term consequences for the business.

The Strategic Plan

When the *strategic plan*, which includes the values, vision, mission and the goals, is complete, it must then be communicated to the rest of the organization. This is called 'cascading', and it should be done one layer at a time and as soon as possible. The process is not complicated, but usually an organization will encounter resistance from some employees who have their heads in the past, and others who are cynical because of how they have been, or are currently being, treated by management. They will go through the classical phases of change outlined in Chapter 1, Change.

Managers must constantly talk about it, ask about it, begin every meeting with it, and relate everything they do to the strategic plan (which we will now refer to as the plan). Some organizations we have worked with have developed fun activities with prizes for employees demonstrating their knowledge of the plan.

When communicating the plan to the lower levels in the organization, there is also a process that should be followed. Some ideas to consider for the meeting are as follows:

- Request the full participation of all employees. The organization should break down by department, function or level. The discussion should be open and honest. Everyone should be allowed their opinion, and if management does not have specific answers, they should admit it.
- Verbalize the process that the management team went through to get to the final plan. Include ideas that management considered and then discarded, and discuss why.
- Discuss the importance of having a clearly articulated strategic plan. Perhaps, encourage ideas from attendees on how they feel their jobs can be enriched by role clarity.
- Have a discussion on how the company is now behaving within the culture and where any gaps might exist.
- Ensure everyone has a copy of the complete document, and has had an opportunity to read it and contribute any input they might have.

The Consequences of Not Developing a Strategic Plan

Many companies and organizations we work with are determined to make a fair return for shareholders, offer a safe, fulfilling workplace for their employees, and deliver quality and value to their customers.

Unfortunately, not all companies strive for these same virtues. Through media reports, we all know of high-profile companies and individual executives whose names have become synonymous with wrongdoing and, in some cases, criminal negligence.

Why are these businesses facing moral corruption and a lack of concern for the constituents they claim to represent? Why are they going down this road and, more importantly, how can it be turned around?

We are pleased that on a regular basis we work with executives who are trying to improve the environment of corporate responsibility. We also see an increased awareness on the part of consumers and investors who are demanding improved social responsibility on the part of the companies from which they buy and in which they invest.

Consequently, many organizations are developing their own strategic plan, which includes a code of conduct and mission statement, and usually it encompasses much more than making a profit.

While these activities are useful, they are not enough. Management must also make an effort to ensure that all employees understand, and are committed to, this ethical way of doing business. As discussed earlier in the chapter, too many companies just write up a code of ethics, dump it on employees without asking for their input, and wait for something to happen.

The other factor that operates in these cases, is that on one hand employees see posters on the walls advertising a wonderful code of conduct and an annual report with wonderful words about a people-oriented and ethical company. On the other hand, if you talk to employees in many of these same organizations, they will not agree that their leaders really adhere to these values, or, in fact, mean them to be followed at all.

When employees feel their expected behavior does not reflect the organization's stated ethics, the organization will ultimately lose psychic energy.

Choosing the People

There is a direct link between organizational culture and performance/effectiveness. This factor is incorporated in a candidate-selection model that we present in some of our workshops. The model was originally developed by our friend Digger, whose story we shared in Chapter 2, Career. It makes the assumption that there are two considerations employed in candidate selection. They are *technical competence* and *fit*.

Technical competence incorporates the acronym **ASK-ART,** and asks the following question:

Does the individual have the

A – aptitudes

S – skills

K – knowledge

to perform the

A – activities

R – roles

T – tasks

required of the job or position?

The "fit" consideration is in keeping with the belief that candidates need to be in the right environment in order to motivate themselves. To determine the right fit the employer should consider these factors: interests, needs, values and feel-good factor (or self-concept).

A fit occurs if the employer deems that the workplace environment and personnel associated with it can:

- stimulate the interests;
- satisfy the needs;
- share the values; and
- enhance the self-esteem of the candidate.

If the employer cannot achieve these four factors, it is unlikely that the candidate, if selected, will remain in the employment offered.

Bridging the Gap

The best way for managers to gain compliance and motivate others is to create an atmosphere of trust. People will follow a manager they know they can trust. This is one of the main criteria for effective leadership.

In our work, we discover that many senior managers are not in touch with what employees believe to be the true operating culture of the organization. To help bridge that gap, we use a survey instrument developed by Human Synergistics® called the Organizational Culture Inventory™ (OCI™).

The company designed the tool to help management accurately assess the culture of the organization. It provides a clear picture of the norms and expectations as perceived by everyone in the organization. The OCI™ is a quantitative instrument that measures 12 sets of norms associated with three general types of organizational cultures: Constructive, Passive/Defensive, and Aggressive/Defensive.

There are two parts to the survey. First the senior management completes the OCI™ Ideal survey. It will give them an assessment of what they believe is the ideal or desired culture required for the organization to succeed in their particular industry. As well, it will provide an assessment of the culture which will attract and retain the most desirable employees.

An appropriate percentage of employees then complete the OCI™ Actual. The instrument will assess what the majority of the employees feel is the actual culture. It provides feedback on how employees are expected to deal with each other, rather than with people outside the organization. It represents the behaviors that people are being consistently rewarded for and those that will result in negative consequences.

The objective is to reduce the gaps between an organization's current culture and its ideal. The exercise will result in an assessment against the 12 sets of norms that describe the thinking and behavioral styles that might implicitly or explicitly be required for people to "fit in" and "meet expectations" in an organization. These behavioral norms specify the way in which all members of an organization, or at least those in similar positions and locations, are expected to approach their work and interact with one another.

The norms also are defined by two underlying dimensions. The first is the extent to which there is a concern for people in the organization, and the other is a concern for task. The second dimension distinguishes between expectations for behaviors directed towards fulfilling the higher-order satisfaction needs and those directed toward protecting and maintaining the lower-order satisfaction needs, that are described on page 98 (Sherren's Hierarchy of Needs).

The OCI™ Circumplex

An organization's scores are plotted on a circular graph known as a Circumplex. The ideal profiles we see generated by the managers of organizations usually indicate a strong preference for high scores in the Constructive categories, moderate to low scores in the Aggressive/Defensive categories, and low scores in the Passive/Defensive categories. Once in awhile, the Passive/Defensive and Aggressive/Defensive ideal norms are reversed for public sector organizations, with the lower scores desired in the Aggressive/Defensive category.

However, quite often what the employees indicate as the actual culture is a more dysfunctional Circumplex. This is where the Constructive styles are proportionally lower than both the Passive/Defensive and Aggressive/Defensive styles. A summary of the styles follows.

Constructive Cultures:

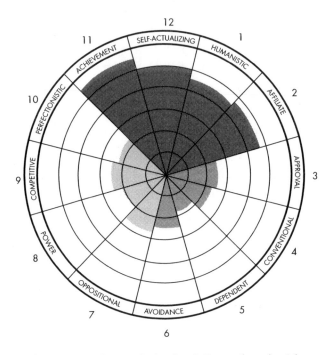

Copyright by Human Synergistics Inc.® Reproduced with permission.

Achievement: Members are expected to set challenging but realistic goals, establish plans to reach those goals, and pursue them with enthusiasm.

Self-actualizing: Members are expected to enjoy their work, develop themselves, and take on new and interesting tasks.

Humanistic: Members are expected to be supportive, constructive, and open to influence in dealing with one another.

Affiliative: Members are expected to be friendly, cooperative, and sensitive to the satisfaction of their work group.

Passive/Defensive Cultures

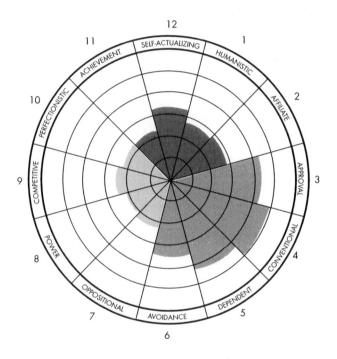

Copyright by Human Synergistics Inc.® Reproduced with permission.

Approval: Employees are expected to agree with, gain the approval of, and be liked by others.

Conventional: Employees are expected to conform, follow the rules, and make a good impression.

Dependent: Employees are expected to do what they are told and clear all decisions with management.

Avoidance: Employees are expected to shift responsibilities to others and avoid any possibility of being blamed for a problem.

Aggressive/Defensive Cultures

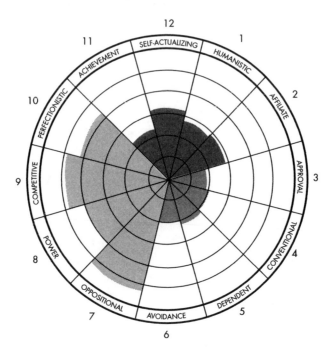

Copyright by Human Synergistics Inc.® Reproduced with permission.

Oppositional: Employees are expected to be critical, oppose the ideas of others, and make safe, low-risk decisions.

Power: Employees are expected to take charge, control others, but do what they are told by managers.

Competitive: Employees are expected to operate in a "win-lose" framework, outperform others, and work against (rather than with) their peers.

Perfectionistic: Employees are expected to appear competent, keep track of everything, and work long hours to attain narrowly defined objectives.

Business leaders today must see that the need for ethics in their organizations is greater than ever before, because social relations, working infrastructures, and technological advancements are more complex and demanding than at any other time in history.

What we have found is that the creation of values, vision and mission will have only marginal effect on the culture of an organization if there is not an absolute determination for implementation on the part of senior management and a complete buy-in and commitment on the part of employees. Senior managers must also put in place appropriate reinforcement processes, to be used when they see employees making decisions that reinforce the desired culture. The behavior must begin at the top, with executives being the role models for the culture.

As well, there must be an alignment of the values to the vision and mission. If not, there will be cultural disconnects which will result in a loss of psychic energy within the organization. People must feel a sense of pride for the organization in which they work. This pride will result in energy, motivation and a sense of connection to all members of the organization.

Many times, the norms that emerge from conducting an OCI™ in an organization do not reflect the statements in the organization's vision and mission. This is because the norms are derived from the reality of what employees face on a day-to-day basis. We have also found that this disconnect will cause role confusion, personal stress, more absenteeism and a higher rate of turnover.

Just as a person will be remembered for the values by which they live, an organization will develop a reputation and a culture based on the choices they make.

The most important choices organizations will be required to make will always be balanced between people and profit.

How Healthy Is Your Culture?

The first step to improving any environment is to determine how healthy the organization's culture is currently. You need to have a measurement of the culture, before you can develop a strategy on how and what to improve. After reading each question, rate your organization's culture on a score of one to five. When you finish, add up your score and review the results.

Never		Sometimes		Always
1	2	3	4	5

1. At work, do you have the opportunity to do what you do best and enjoy? _____
2. Do you have the resources necessary to meet expectations? _____
3. Do you know what is expected of you at work? _____
4. Does the environment allow you the freedom to do your best work? _____
5. Does your manager take a genuine interest in your career development? _____
6. Are your organization's values, mission and strategic objectives articulated clearly? _____
7. Are your personal goals and values being met in your workplace? _____
8. Does management value your opinions and suggestions? _____
9. In the last six months, has your manager talked to you about your progress? _____
10. In the last month, have you received recognition or praise for doing good work? _____
11. Does your environment encourage and support learning opportunities? _____

12. Does your environment support a balance
    between work and personal life?   _____

   Enter your total points here: _____

   Results

   40 or above: Good news! You have a healthy culture. You can be a catalyst to maintain and improve the work environment. You will also improve your own emotional and physical health within a healthy culture.

   Below 40: Review your current culture and determine how you can influence the development of a healthier environment. Take every opportunity to suggest or contribute new ways to promote a healthier culture.

   Add your own: There may be other positive aspects of your culture, which these questions did not cover, yet are contributing to a healthy environment. Feel free to list these factors below. Score these factors and add the points to your results.

   Additional factors that contribute to a healthy workplace:

   _____

   _____

   _____

   _____

   _____

Coaching

Encourage and Reinforce
Human Performance

**Coaching is a way of working with people that leaves
them more competent and more fulfilled so that they
are more able to contribute to their organizations
and find meaning in what they are doing.**
James Flaherty
Coaching and Leadership Trainer
Author, *Coaching: Evoking Excellence in Others*

Why Consider Coaching?

The process of coaching is the most important interaction a manager can have with an employee and an essential element in our Vitamin C approach to a healthy workplace. Here are some of the reasons managers should consider coaching:

- to acclimate a new employee to their role within the organization;
- to enable people to cope with change within an organization that is experiencing significant restructuring;

- to help a valued employee deal with a problem;
- to determine the developmental and career needs of the employee;
- to help an employee reclaim their value by improving performance and personal satisfaction;
- to sharpen and sustain an employee's competitive advantage;
- to develop long-term excellent performance and sustained development;
- to more easily achieve the alignment of the passions of employees with the mission of the organization.

Coaching will contribute to an organization's bottom line. Proper coaching will result in highly competent, productive and constructive employees. Effective coaching is one of the major contributing factors in keeping talented people and it will substantially reduce turnover. Incorrect coaching will result in employees acting either passive or aggressive, and ultimately in inhibiting their personal development and potential.

The main purpose of coaching is to enable ordinary employees to achieve extraordinary things.

Coaching Tips

- Have an open mind.
- Do *your* homework.
- Clarify expectations.
- "Make" the time.
- Be dedicated and *seriously* committed.
- Incorporate your own experiences and knowledge.

Employee Motivation

True leaders have discovered that employee motivation comes not from lighting a fire beneath them, but by creating a fire within them.

People do things for their own reasons, not yours. Therefore you cannot "motivate" someone else. You can only work to create conditions that will encourage them to motivate themselves in desirable ways.

Before you can truly understand the dynamics of coaching, you must understand what really motivates people. A number of years ago Abraham Maslow made famous his theory on motivation. His theory is known as the "hierarchy of needs."

He said that at the base of the motivation for every individual were their physiological needs – food, shelter, clothing. Basically, his idea was that if you were starving to death, you would swim through a swamp full of alligators to get food. But he added a profound thought. "Once a need is met, it ceases to become a motivator." He believed that once you get a sufficient amount of food, not only would you not swim through the swamp, you would not even live near the swamp.

Then you would rise to the next level in the hierarchy, which he described as safety and security. Once that need has been met, you would progress to the need for social interaction. We are basically all social animals and want to be connected to others. Once that need has been met you would progress to the ego need – to achieve your 15 minutes of fame in life. With that in hand, finally you would rise to the top of the pyramid, which he defined as self-actualization.

The second profound thing Maslow said was that if any need is blocked, a person will focus all his or her energy on the one immediately below the one that is blocked. For instance, if you had a sufficient amount of food, and your need for safety and security was blocked, you would go down one level in the hierarchy and focus on stockpiling food.

Although this is a fascinating and valid theory, it is hard for managers to relate this to motivating employees in the workplace. Consequently, Joe Sherren came up with his own motivational hierarchy, which helped us better understand organizational dynamics. What Joe discovered was that at the base of motivation for people who worked for him was the need to "get or keep a job." He found that new employees would sincerely promise to do almost anything required, just for the opportunity to be hired or maintain their position.

Once that need was intrinsically met, however, it ceased to be a motivator. Then people would move on to the next higher level, which he describes as "opportunity for growth and development." At the second level, when managers asked them to go out of their way, to work on a long weekend or assist in an urgent situation, for example, employees would want to know if their efforts would result in potential promotions or new and challenging projects. If they came to believe that their efforts would indeed be met with positive results, the need ceased to be a motivator and they would naturally move to the next level, "peer respect."

At this point, employees would perform primarily to impress and gain the recognition and respect of the people with whom they work. When they have gained that respect, it would cease to be a motivator and they would go on to the next higher level, "recognition and respect from management." This strong and important need must be satisfied in order for any employee to feel needed and to develop a desire to succeed. Once met, an employee would then progress to the top of the pyramid of motivation, which is an employee's desire for "personal achievement."

An illustration of this model follows.

Sherren's Hierarchy of Needs©

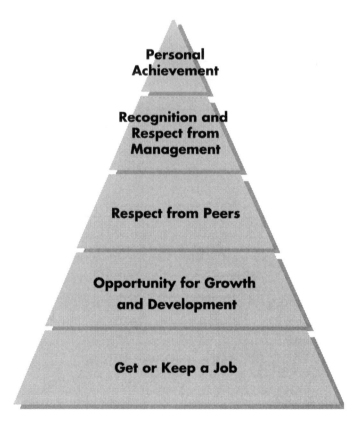

Remember, the second thing that Maslow said was that if any need was blocked, people would regress to the next lower order in the hierarchy. Joe's model works the same way. If any of these motivation factors are blocked, an employee will regress. For instance, if an employee felt secure in their job and ready to progress to the next level, but found that opportunity for growth, development and any possibility of a more challenging assignment was not possible, they would regress to the previous motivation level and go looking for another job somewhere else.

Likewise, if the need for recognition and respect from management was blocked, the employees would focus on their need for respect from peers. Employees would get together with other employees, meet for lunch, drinks or in coffee shops to have "bitch sessions." In some cases, it could even become an attempt to turn all employees against management. Ultimately, this could result in an organized employee movement against all management.

Managers must realize that if employees do not receive the respect and recognition they feel is due, just and deserved, they will find other outlets to satisfy this need, and it will be with each other, collectively.

The Ideal Employee

In our training sessions we ask managers to shout out their answers to the following question. "If you had someone you felt was a high-potential employee, deserving a promotion or higher responsibility, what are some of the words you would use to describe him or her?" As they shout out the words, we put them in two columns. Following are some samples of these thoughts.

(A)	(B)
Experience	Self-motivated
Decision maker	Enthusiastic
Shows judgment	Cooperative
Trained	Committed
Innovative	Flexible
Proven track record	Self-confident

Column A lists those items that indicate employees can do the job, while column B represents those attributes that show they want to and are eager to do the job. When we ask on which column does a manager have more direct control, we invariably get the answer "A." We then point out that as managers, they have exactly the same ability to influence both columns.

You will gain more information on this concept in "The Competent Bike Rider," found later in this chapter.

Focus on Strengths

Some managers seem to have the natural ability to build healthy coaching relationships. They are sensitive to their employees' needs, and they focus on what they do well in order to help them perform even better. Other managers are more concerned about their personal agenda, and thus focus on the negative aspects and what their employees do wrong.

As we said earlier in our introduction, our goal with this book, and our speeches and workshops, is to help create a healthy workplace. That would be a workplace where people are doing what they love to do, and doing it in an environment that supports and encourages the development of their strengths.

Part of that process involves helping managers become more positive and supportive coaches. In our experience the process of making this happen becomes easier when the manager is able to focus on the employees' strengths, while coaching them to manage their weaknesses. One of the best books written about this subject is entitled *Soar With Your Strengths*. The authors, Donald Clifton and Paula Nelson, begin their book with a parable about a rabbit that goes to school in order to become smarter. Over the past couple of years, we have used and adapted this parable when speaking to organizations about focusing on the behaviors that will bring success. With some poetic license, we have adapted the parable here.

There once was a rabbit that attended a school offering courses on how to become a well-rounded animal. The courses included running, swimming, tree climbing and flying.

In the first course, the rabbit was a star. He felt very good running over the hills and down the valleys as fast as he could go. In fact, with the strong muscles in his rear legs, he was the fastest in the class. The instructor said that he would be able to run even faster with some training. He felt fabulous.

One evening, he told his parents how much fun he thought the school was. They told him how proud they were, and said that he would be an even better animal after he learned all those other skills. They also felt wonderful.

The next day the course concentrated on swimming. The instructor told the rabbit to jump in the water. Being a brave rabbit, he jumped in. Unfortunately, no matter how hard he tried to swim, he kept sinking. The instructor pulled him out, just as he was starting to panic. He left school that day a very disheartened and unhappy rabbit.

After sharing his disappointment with his parents, he felt better. They encouraged him to try again. They told him that they believed in him and that he could do anything he set his mind to. They also made it clear that they wanted him to be successful and to graduate, and that meant completing all the courses.

At this point the rabbit decided to get some help. So he went to see a coach. After some assessments and testing, the coach announced that he understood the problem. He suggested that since the rabbit could run so very well, he didn't need to take those classes anymore, but he would arrange for him to have more swimming classes.

As soon as he heard that suggestion, the rabbit just gave up!

The moral of this story is that too often in the workplace, managers tell employees, "You are not good enough, unless you change." Change, in this case, means working on your weaknesses. Managers may tell you to just work harder, or they may suggest that you go for remedial training in order to overcome your weaknesses. Unfortunately, if you become focused only on weaknesses, you will be wasting a great deal of energy. The practice of focusing only on weaknesses begins to suffocate your strengths. Focusing on the failures in your workplace tends to make you feel terrible and puts you in a frame of mind in which you will inevitably neglect the successes.

The greatest chance for creating a healthy coaching relationship with employees lies in remembering and improving on the good things (sometimes this means helping them to get 'back on track'), while doing fewer of the bad things. As Paula and Donald suggest in *Soar With Your Strengths*, "If you develop your strengths to the maximum, the strength becomes so great it overwhelms the weaknesses."

Instead of thinking about what is wrong with the person, identify and develop what is right.

The Invincible Coach

Think about what coaching would be like if you devoted more time to discovering what you and your employees appreciate and enjoy. Imagine spending most of your time working on the good stuff until the positive experiences simply overwhelmed the negative ones.

We just love the story about the Chinese table-tennis player competing in the 1984 Olympics. It seems this particular player had a major weakness. He couldn't play with his backhand. Consequently, he played with only his forehand. His competition was aware of the fact and the other coaches instructed their players to go for his backhand.

"Get the ball there and you've got him beat. He won't be able to return it!" they advised. The other players followed the advice. Player after player won a point whenever they played the ball to his backhand.

Unfortunately for them, they just couldn't get the ball to his backhand often enough to make a difference. The Chinese player won the gold medal. You see, he was playing with his strength. When the coach of the Chinese team was interviewed and asked about his training method, he replied, "We practice eight hours a day perfecting our strengths." He knew instinctively that if his player's strong forehand became even stronger, it would overwhelm his weak backhand.

Imagine what a coaching session would be like if your manager focused on what was right with your work, and the discussion was centered around how to make it even better.

The answer lies in encouraging and reinforcing those things that people do best, while coaching them to manage the things they don't do well.

If you want an invincible coaching relationship, one that cannot be beaten, then focus on and develop individual strengths.

Leaders should be wary of the phrase, *Let me show you how,* when coaching a team member through a new task. When in a rush, it's tempting to demonstrate a task rather than to provide supportive direction. The real motivation behind *Let me show you how* is usually to get the work done rather than to help the team member learn.

This may boost short-term performance, but will inevitably hurt long-term proficiency. Before you demonstrate a task, ask yourself the following questions.

1. Am I supporting the team member or helping myself?
2. Will my demonstration increase or decrease their independence?

The Importance of Feedback in Coaching

"Feedback" is a way of helping another person to consider changing their behavior. It is communication with a person (or a group), which gives that person information about how he/she affects others. As in a guided missile system, feedback helps an individual keep their behavior "on target" and, thus, better achieve their goals. Some criteria for useful feedback includes the following:

1. **It is descriptive rather than evaluative.** By describing one's own reaction, it leaves the individual free to use it or not as they see fit. By avoiding evaluative language, the manager reduces the need for the individual to react defensively.

2. **It is specific rather than general.** If a manager tells an employee that they are "dominating," it will probably not be as useful to him or her as to be told that "just now when we were discussing the issue, you did not listen to what others said and I felt forced to accept your arguments or face attack from you."

3. **It takes into account the needs of both the receiver and giver of feedback.** Feedback can be destructive when it serves only one's own needs and fails to consider the needs of the person on the receiving end.

4. **It is directed toward behavior that the receiver can do something about.** Frustration is only increased when a person is reminded of some shortcoming over which they have no control.

5. **It is solicited, rather than imposed.** Feedback is most useful when the receiver has formulated the kind of question which those observing him/her can answer.

6. **It is well-timed.** In general, feedback is most useful at the earliest opportunity after the given behavior. This depends, of course, on the person's readiness to hear it, along with such variables as support available from others.

7. **It is checked to insure clear communication.** One way of checking for clear communication is to have the receiver try to rephrase the feedback he/she received to see if it corresponds to what the sender had in mind.

8. **It is checked for accuracy.** When feedback is given in a training group, both giver and receiver have an opportunity to check

with others in the group, the accuracy of the feedback. Within the group it's easier to determine if the feedback is only one person's impression or an impression shared by others.

Feedback, then, is a way of giving help. It is a corrective mechanism for the individual who wants to learn how well their behavior matches their intentions. It can also act as a means for establishing one's identity—perhaps helpful in answering *Who am I?*

Dynamic Coaching

Coaching is a process, not an event. The process can be powerful in that it unlocks the potential of an individual and maximizes their performance. The theory of dynamic coaching is based on the belief that one can be most effective by tailoring one's behavior to meet the demands of the situation and the needs of the employee. The process involves the coach determining the level of competence of the employee, where they want to be, and what they need to do to get there. It also consists of different phases, with each one influencing the type of coaching intervention.

Our colleague, Karen Lee, approaches the coaching concept with the following opinion in mind: "A person is a process not a product."

People have the capacity to learn new concepts and build new skills from birth to death. In our world of work, and even in life in general, anything that another person says or does to us has an impact on:

* **our self-esteem**—the love we have for ourselves with or without "warts";
* **our self-confidence**—our belief in our ability to contribute in a meaningful way;

- **our sense of identity**—who we believe we are, for example, intelligent, friendly, outgoing.

A manager or supervisor has tremendous power to affect any or all of these pieces of self. Consequently, a manager who disciplines a person in front of others affects all of the pieces. A trainer who shows impatience when a person is a little slow to learn affects all of the pieces. In the same way, a parent who tells his/her child he or she is stupid affects all of the pieces.

Two key questions are commonly evident when it comes to the productivity of human beings. They are: Can I do it? *and* Will I do it?

Leaders, by definition, are people who influence the behavior of others. They have a profound responsibility to influence positively. They should do their best to enhance and maintain self-esteem, self-confidence and sense of identity in the people for whom they are responsible, without detracting from any of the fundamental human pieces. Let's put Karen's thoughts and our concepts into a practical, application.

The process we use is both simple and effective. The successful implementation, however, is more difficult. In it, a lot depends on your ability to assess the level of motivation and the competence of employees. You will discover that you need to take extreme care at each phase in the type of coaching behavior you apply.

Accepting the premise that your objective is to have employees who are highly competent, motivated and enthusiastic, let us illustrate a model, which will help you achieve this result. Joe has developed the process by building on many of the theories and models that other experts in the field of leadership have created and evolved.

The Competent Bike Rider

To describe the process, we will use an analogy. There are other numerous stories we could use. The one we find striking a chord with most people is the one that takes them back to the time when they had the opportunity to teach a child to ride a bicycle, whether it was a son, daughter, little brother, little sister or even a neighborhood child.

Go back to that point in time. Try to remember the first phase of this process when the child came to you and said, "Buy me a bike, I really want a bike." In response, you may have pointed out that they couldn't ride a bike. Invariably, a keen child would answer, "Yes I can, oh yes, I can." If parents took this enthusiasm at face value, they might actually go out, purchase an expensive bike and give it to the child saying, "Here, go ride it." If, in fact, they did that, the child would probably respond, "I really can't. I need you to teach me," thus showing a reluctance or unwillingness to independently get on the bike and enthusiastically ride it down the street.

Later on we are going to relate this analogy to what happens in the process of working with an employee and taking them through their competency stages. The similarity with the child stretching the truth about their bicycle-riding abilities is akin to how people will tend to exaggerate their abilities and experiences on their resumés.

Remember, the outcome you are looking for is to have a child who is a knowledgeable, skilled, safe, enthusiastic, flexible, self-motivated, independent bicycle rider—in short, one about whom you do not have to worry. In order to accomplish this in the workplace, you must understand the different styles of leadership that are available.

Over the past 50 years, many management consultants and behavioral psychologists have been developing theories and mapping the different styles that managers use. Each of the theories builds on the previous one, and takes it to a new level. Great work has been done by McGregor, Fielden, Maslow, Korman, Blake and Mouton, Hershey, Blanchard, Hertzberg and Lafferty. Joe has taken the sum of this work and moved it one more step in its evolution to help managers understand why they must modify their coaching style to be more effective.

Quite simply, many management gurus approached managers' behavior using a two-dimensional concept. One dimension concerns the extent to which leaders engage in task-oriented behaviors. Those may result in high- or low-directive coaching. The second dimension that leaders could use in coaching is high interpersonal and relationship behaviors, or low interpersonal and relationship behaviors. In a model, these two dimensions cover four major coaching behaviors. We call it the socio-emotional focus.

1. High directive and low interpersonal
2. High directive and high interpersonal
3. Low directive and high interpersonal
4. Low directive and low interpersonal

Correspondingly, employees' competency is determined by two dimensions. The first is ability. Can they do the job? The second concerns eagerness. Do they want to do the job? There are four levels of employee competency.

1. Unable and reluctant
2. Unable and eager
3. Able and reluctant
4. Able and eager

On one hand, a person's ability is determined by their education, experience, training, track record, knowledge, innovative thinking, ability to plan, creativity, task skills, and their decision-making judgment. On the other hand, the "want to" effects that will determine an employee's eagerness include self-confidence, self-motivation, enthusiasm, commitment, assertiveness, co-operation, activity level and flexibility.

With our bicycle rider, our goal is to have a young person who is a highly competent bicycle rider, or one who both can and will ride the bike (able and eager). In order to achieve this, a parent or adult instinctively knows exactly the correct sequence of behaviors in which they must engage.

We use these great leadership abilities in many other daily aspects of our lives, such as raising our children, coaching a minor league team, coordinating Scouts, or even in our volunteer roles. However, in an organizational or corporate setting, when we are promoted to management, we do not always consider what we inherently know is great leadership, and instead engage in behaviors that we have been conditioned to believe are the right things to do.

Let us now return to our developing bicycle rider. At this point we have determined they are unable and fairly reluctant to get on that bike on their own and independently ride it down the street. We call this phase *Competency 1*. Do not mistake this reluctance as an unwillingness to actually become a great bicycle rider. It is simply an insecurity and psychological lack of confidence experienced at this particular point in time.

In surveying the situation, you may ask, "What coaching style should the adult use?" The response is often "high interpersonal and low directive." But if you actually went up to the child at that point and gave them lots of socio-emotional, supportive behavior, told them how well they were going to do, encouraged them not to worry and praised them for taking this important step, they would still not be able (or confident) to get on the bicycle and ride it. What they require at this time is lots of "high directive" behavior and communication.

In a fairly straightforward and directive voice, the adult would instruct them to sit on the seat, put their left foot on one peddle, put their right on the other, and put both hands on the handle bars. Then, the adult would advise them to follow specific instructions as he or she started to push the bike down the street. With the activity, the parent would continue to give the child lots of direction and some assurances, or a little bit of interpersonal, to reassure the child that the parent will not allow them to fall or get hurt. We refer to the high directive, low interpersonal coaching style as *instructing*.

As the adult continued to push the child down the street, instructing them on what to do next, he or she would observe that the child was actually starting to follow the instructions—and achieving some small accomplishments. Then the adult would probably start engaging in some mild encouragement, increasing it as the child became even more proficient.

After the adult had run up and down the street a couple of dozen times, pushing the bike while continuing to instruct and increasing the feedback, they would become tired and perhaps say, "Let's take a rest now." At this point, the child might reply, "No, lets keep going." While the child would be showing high enthusiasm and confidence, he or she would still not be "able." We refer to the stage as *Competency 2.*

The style the adult must engage in, at this point, would be both "high interpersonal" and "high directive." It is the style that requires the most sensitivity and effort on the part of the adult—and it is the most energy draining.

The "interpersonal" behavior would come in the form of encouragement and compliments on how well the child was doing. The highly "directive" behavior would come in the form of explaining. Such direction might take the form of explaining the importance of taking a rest, explaining the consequences of not taking one step at a time, or explaining the importance of understanding the big picture. We call this coaching style *guiding*.

After an appropriate rest, the child would get back on the bicycle and together they would review some of the things learned. The adult would continue the encouragement and explain some additional skills, until the child got to the point where the adult knew that the child was now able.

Please make no mistake, it is the adult's responsibility to decide when the child is actually able. The same holds true in organizations.

It is the manager's responsibility to determine when the employee is able.

Once this point is reached in the bicycle scenario, the adult would say, "I am going to let go now." The child would respond loudly, "NO." At this point, an interesting transition takes place. When people develop from the "can't do" but eager stage, and go to the "can do" stage, they regress to becoming reluctant, showing an insecurity and lack of confidence. We call this stage *Competency 3*.

At this point, low directive but extremely high interpersonal behavior is required of the adult who should give a lot of support, encourage and build the child's confidence. They could do this by asking questions, reassuring the child, perhaps by saying, "I let go three times already, and you did not even notice." They would also make the child comfortable and lend support by saying, "I'll run beside you for a little while." We call this third coaching style *inspiring*, because that *is* what the parent is doing, inspiring the person to take the next big step towards their development and independence—a step that requires the acceptance of some risk.

Finally, as the child would gain the proficiency to wobble away, the adult would stand and applaud, shout encouragement, perhaps call the spouse to come out, and maybe even the neighbors. Some parents have even been known to go get a video camera. Once again, all these behaviors inspire the child to try even harder.

After the child had been riding the bicycle for a few months, the child would soon show that he or she was quite able and very eager, having reached the *Competency 4* stage. The adult's style would now be to leave them alone. We call this fourth coaching style *empowering*. This is not only low in directive behavior, but also low in interpersonal behavior. And it would remain so, other than to encourage a little when positive behavior was observed such as attention to safety and care for the bicycle.

These steps are the secret to being a true and dynamic leader. Every employee goes through this same set of attitudes and behaviors and they must be coached appropriately at each of these stages. Using the appropriate coaching styles will not only result in highly competent employees, but indeed employees who enjoy their job, enjoy coming to work, are loyal to the organization and who trust management.

However, do you believe that is the way most of us are coached at work by our bosses? Most will answer "no." We have observed that the way many of us are coached is, we are instructed very specifically on what to do, how to do it, and when it should be done. The manager many times even repeats the instructions. Then we are left alone to complete the responsibility, or empowered. If we make a mistake, or do not get the desired results, we are instructed again and left alone once again.

If adults used this same process in teaching children to ride a bike—told them what to do (put you hands here, feet here, keep your balance and peddle hard), then let the child go—the result would be the child crashing to the ground. Using a process similar to that which happens between manager and employees, the adult would instruct them again, this time talking slower. Again it would end in disastrous results. The third time the parent would shout at them, or put them on a performance appraisal review.

If, in fact, we coached our children this way we would end up with kids who are poor bicycle riders, or those who would have very little motivation to ride a bicycle. More importantly, these young people would not have any trust in the parent and could become wary of any other responsibility the parent might want them to take on.

It's well worth noting that the same thing happens at work, when we coach our employees using only the instructing and empowering styles. We end up with people who are not motivated to take responsibility and who have very little trust in management.

Following is a chart that outlines the competency stages and the coaching style each requires.

Employee Competence	Coaching Style
Unable and reluctant	Instructing
Unable and eager	Guiding
Able and reluctant	Inspiring
Able and eager	Empowering

As employees develop through each of these competency levels, their level of motivation also evolves through the hierarchy described earlier. Following are illustrations of the behaviors and levels we have been discussing.

Dynamic Coaching©

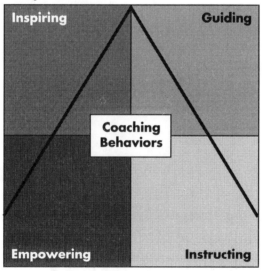

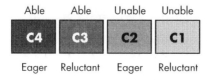

Managers should not count on finding top quality, self-motivated, enthusiastic and competent employees. Such individuals are usually scarce and hard to find. The test of a good manager is to make ordinary people perform better than what seems to be their capability, to bring out the strengths they have, and to use each employee's own internal desires to inspire them to greatness.

The role of a manager is to develop competent employees. But, *what competencies are important for employees to have?* Human Synergistics® has determined that there are 14 competencies that companies need to have in order to succeed. The first was compiled through a survey asking chief executive officers of North America's leading corporations what competencies they felt were most important for success. They are categorized as:

- task skills;
- interpersonal skills; and
- personal skills.

The skills are further broken down into 14 key functional areas, as in the following.

Task Skills

Problem Solving: Recognizing and Solving Problems
This skill involves:
- recognizing and analyzing problems;
- dealing with 'competing' issues;
- approaching unforeseen circumstances;
- selecting unpopular or risky courses of action;
- reacting to complicated problems and situations;
- working with others to solve complex problems.

Time Management: Allocating Time and Using It Effectively

This skill involves:

- allocating time to the proper things;
- dealing with the relationship between when things should be done and when they are done;
- making estimates regarding the amount of time needed to complete a task;
- 'clearing up' identified problems in a timely manner;
- making sure that important issues are covered in meetings and discussions;
- staying focused on critical activities;
- pacing the workday.

Planning: Providing Direction and Scheduling Activities

This skill involves:

- developing detailed plans;
- delineating and documenting the steps needed to implement a decision;
- anticipating events and specifying appropriate courses of action;
- making plans regarding tasks people are to accomplish on a daily basis;
- defining priorities or major steps to be taken when introducing a change or new project;
- developing and communicating strategies to deal with unforeseen consequences.

Goal Setting: Establishing Goals and Objectives

This skill involves:

- setting objectives for the work group or unit;
- focusing objectives on issues employees can control;
- establishing specific, concrete and clear objectives;
- setting objectives well ahead of decisions about who is going to do what;

- developing measurable and quantifiable objectives;
- clearly specifying priorities;
- using goals and objectives to actively monitor performance.

Performance Leadership: Motivating Performance and Personal Development

This skill involves:

- structuring employees' work to make it motivating and interesting;
- evaluating performance by providing a sense of accomplishment and direction;
- assigning challenging work;
- motivating employees to maximize quality and quantity of work;
- setting challenging, reasonable and fair performance standards;
- recognizing and regarding good performance;
- tailoring rewards to personal needs and interests.

Organizing: Assigning Responsibilities and Coordinating Tasks

This skill involves:

- minimizing duplication of effort;
- assigning authority to others that is clear and appropriate to their job responsibilities;
- giving people the authority necessary to meet their responsibilities;
- organizing tasks to ensure that those responsible have the necessary resources;
- assigning tasks to those who are most qualified;
- assigning people the tasks that complement their existing activities;
- ensuring that the tasks performed by your staff 'fit together'.

Interpersonal Skills

Team Development: Promoting Teamwork and Cooperation

This skill involves:

- creating a cooperative work 'climate';
- helping people work together toward shared objectives;
- developing individual work goals in relation to group goals;
- encouraging group members to pitch in and help one another;
- promoting group discussion and collaboration;
- focusing on the progress of the group and members' contributions when monitoring individual performance;
- designing and organizing special assignments and new projects around teams.

Delegation: Decentralizing and Empowering Others

This skill involves:

- assuming a general approach to tasks and allowing work group members to draw up the specifics;
- giving people the freedom to determine how to get the job done;
- allowing group members to decide who does what;
- emphasizing general guidelines when assigning tasks, then enabling people to proceed using their own judgment;
- giving employees the autonomy and flexibility to respond to problems;
- using plans and strategies in a flexible way to allow people to make changes and respond to unanticipated events.

Participation: Sharing Power and Involving Others

This skill involves:

- evaluating suggestions on the basis of merit, not the source;
- being open to ideas from others;

- helping people feel free to share their opinions and perspectives;
- making decisions affecting the work group after sharing and seeking information from people in the group;
- sincerely asking how things are going, acknowledging difficulties, and factoring them into your decisions;
- making decisions involving different ways of doing things in consultation with those responsible for making the change;
- addressing complex problems by encouraging the participation of those with the necessary information and expertise.

Integrating Differences: Accepting and Resolving Conflicts

This skill involves:

- approaching work group arguments by deciding what is correct based on facts, instead of on who holds what position;
- treating disagreements as healthy expressions of different viewpoints;
- allowing disagreements to be expressed as a means of generating ideas and improving things;
- disagreeing with others by paying attention to their ideas and openly sharing your own;
- handling differences of opinion by questioning others to explore reasons for the differences;
- working on conflicts by paying equal concern to the needs of others and your own needs;
- mediating disagreements by reducing the sources of conflict, misunderstandings or communication breakdowns, for example.

Providing Feedback: Facilitating and Encouraging Growth

This skill involves:

- being helpful and supportive when talking to others about their work;

- discussing performance by complimenting the good and helping to improve weaker areas;
- helping others to grow and develop by providing constructive feedback on a regular basis;
- providing support and understanding when people make mistakes;
- focusing on others' strengths that can be developed in specific ways;
- offering feedback and advice that emphasizes things the recipient can do something about.

Personal Skills

Stress Processing: Managing Crises and Reducing Stress

This skill involves:

- seeking and discussing all suggestions calmly and openly when under stress or dealing with a crisis;
- solving a complicated problem by staying in control, using the information available and making a rational decision;
- reacting to things 'going wrong' by calmly trying to correct the situation;
- coping with the unexpected by remaining in good humor and working on the problem until it's resolved;
- addressing a buildup of little problems by staying objective and working to resolve each issue;
- putting aside stressful situations and moving on to the next activity;
- interacting with others and approaching your work in a way that minimizes stress for yourself and others.

Maintaining Integrity: Gaining the Trust and Confidence of Others

This skill involves:

- keeping your word and commitments;

- speaking the truth and being believable;
- respecting confidences;
- 'telling it like it is';
- supporting and implementing decisions agreed upon in conversation or formal meetings;
- using your influence appropriately to represent the concerns of your employees and to promote their interests;
- sharing the credit with group members when your work group carries out an assignment particularly well.

Commitment: Demonstrating Loyalty and Responsibility

This skill involves:

- accepting heavy workloads without complaint;
- expressing trust and confidence in the organization and top management;
- applying oneself virtually all the time and giving a great amount to the job;
- doing anything to help in an emergency or when problems arise;
- setting an excellent example of dedication to the job;
- emphasizing the larger organization when setting objectives, establishing priorities and interpreting organizational strategies for your work group;
- supporting proposals that would benefit the organization, regardless of their effect on your career objectives.

There are four competencies which Human Synergistics® have determined to be essential for a manager to provide effective coaching. These are as follows:

> Providing Feedback
> Performance Leadership
> Delegation
> Goal Setting

The originators have indicated that these are essential, because they capture the essence of a manager's attitude and skill towards the growth and development of others.

Human Synergistics® has a 360° survey process known as MEPS™ (Management Effectiveness Profile System™), which can be used to assess these competencies in managers. This system also provides a step-by-step method of personal development that can be used by managers to increase their skills in these critical areas.

> *The mediocre teacher tells*
> *The good teacher explains*
> *The superior teacher demonstrates*
> *The great teacher inspires*
> William Arthur Ward

We believe that sensational coaches do it all!

Bosses Who Did Not Care

In a recent incident that garnered widespread media attention, a woman was attacked in a company parking lot. She was left lying unconscious within eyesight of a nearby company. However, when empoyees of that company asked if they could go and assist, their boss told them not to get involved, and indicated that they were not allowed to leave their workstations during company time. Afterwards, the employees did go to assist the woman, and she was taken to the hospital.

Completing the MEPS™

If you would like to complete one of the MEPS™ (*Management Effectiveness Profile System™*), please contact the authors directly by e-mail at: joe@ethos.on.ca or luke@thecouplescoach.com. For further information, these instruments are also available by contacting Human Synergistics® by phone at 519-284-4135 or e-mail: info@hscanada.ca.

MEPS™ (Management Effectiveness Profile System™). All rights reserved.

When we first read the story we thought, "This is different," but it isn't. In his book *The Corporate Coach*, Jim Miller asked for entries for a "Worst Boss" contest. He received over 1000 entries from employees who thought their boss was "lower than a snake's belly." Here are just a few examples of the practices noted by employees:

- Hiding or altering an employee's time card;
- Searching employees' lockers and personal belongings;
- Verbally abusing employees until they started to cry.

One of the most shocking was a letter from a worker who said the boss had refused to call 911 before 5:00 p.m. to look after an employee who had died at his desk. It would disrupt the office and be unproductive, the manager reasoned.

In our own surveys, we have found that a good manager can actually be the greatest long-term motivator of employees. An *Industry Week* study found that "a manager with vision and values" was an employee's top motivator. The results are consistent with many other studies we have seen and comments we continue to receive from participants in our programs.

What Is Your Coaching IQ?

The following exercise will help you to rate your coaching behavior, and determine how much effort you are putting into developing your employees. After reading each question, give yourself a score of one to five. When you are finished, add up your score and see how you compare with the results listed on the next page.

Never		Sometimes		Always
1	2	3	4	5

1. Do you clarify your role and your expectations? _____
2. When you begin the coaching session, do you put the employee at ease? _____
3. Do you take the time to build trust? _____
4. Do you stay attentive and focused during the coaching session? _____
5. Do you provide appropriate support and training when needed? _____
6. Do employees report they feel you hear and understand them? _____
7. Do you ask open-ended questions to encourage an employee's opinion or suggestions? _____
8. Do you refrain from pigeonholing employees? _____
9. Do you respond authentically to employees without using techniques or canned answers? _____
10. Do you explore new possibilities or refrain from offering your solution to a problem? _____
11. Are you a good role model? _____
12. Do you provide feedback in a timely manner? _____

Enter your total points here: _____

Results

40 or above: Congratulations. You are a competent coach who shows a genuine interest in the development of your employees. Continue to practice these coaching behaviors and you will further contribute to a healthy workplace.

Below 40: Review what coaching skills you do well. Determine what coaching skills you could learn and determine which of these you would be willing to practice and improve. Every time you increase your coaching skills you are contributing to a healthy workplace. Listen to others, and they will listen to you.

Add your own: There may be other coaching skills that you practice that are not described in the previous exercise. Add any skills that you believe would improve your coaching relationship. Feel free to list these skills below. Score these skills and add the points to your results.

My coaching skills examples:

_____

_____

_____

_____

_____

Communication

Understand and Be Understood

**The greatest motivational act one person
can do for another is to listen.**
Roy Moody
Seminar and workshop leader on topics
such as coaching and teamwork

The Business Case

If our focus is to become more professional in this rapidly changing, hi-tech world, we must be even more vigilant about maintaining responsive communications with all the people who are important to our success.

Most of the activities at work depend on our ability to understand and apply effective interpersonal communication. This is true in acquiring information, giving information, offering services to clients, and teamwork with colleagues, subordinates and managers.

Maximizing our potential to communicate more efficiently is paramount. Many employers greatly value strong communicators. In surveys, executives have said that they value interpersonal skills as much as technical skills. With an eye on the bottom line, they are sensitive to the fact that a great deal of money is wasted because instructions are misunderstood.

Effective interpersonal communication also plays a major role in retention management. The reason often cited by people who leave their jobs is that their boss didn't understand them. People leaving their jobs often express concerns such as, "My boss never listens to me," or "He tunes me out whenever I start talking."

The Personal Case

Communication is the most important skill in life. The ability to communicate is absolutely critical to our effectiveness. Aside from the fact that in today's competitive work environment strong communicators will have the edge, improving our communication skills will help us to meet some basic human needs.

One of our strongest desires is to be understood. To have another person understand what we think, feel, value, love, hate, fear, believe in and are committed to, can be one of life's greatest pleasures. That is why we believe that effective interpersonal communication is such an important part of a healthy workplace.

Effective interpersonal communication is also necessary to satisfy our need for recognition. The way our manager, peers and subordinates communicate with us lets us determine how we are accepted and appreciated. It is this kind of communication that determines our *fit* within an organization. In fact, it has often been said that it is the fit that determines whether a person is hired or fired. Unfortunately, as we hear from many attendees in our sessions, effective communication in the workplace is rare.

Aside from the fact that the way we communicate directly affects the bottom line, and whether or not we retain our star performers, it also plays a very important role in our physical well-being. The psychological need to be understood is important for our survival. Research has shown that a lack of adult interpersonal relationships can contribute to hypertension and coronary disease.

We also know that our work will suffer when we have trouble communicating effectively with our co-workers. In fact, poor communication is one of the chief causes of stress-related problems in the workplace. It actually determines the kind of work relationship we have, and whether or not our basic needs will be met.

One of the basic needs that can be met through effective communication is our need to reduce uncertainty. We communicate to create a shared understanding of what is most important to us. As we learn more about our co-workers, and they learn more about us, we are both better able to understand and predict each other's behavior. This helps the world become a more stable place, safer and more certain.

Effective Communication Reduces Stress

Stress is a killer. It's simple. Therefore, anything you can do to reduce the negative stress in your workplace and to increase your resistance to stress will definitely increase your health and your lifespan. In case you are not familiar with how our body responds to stress, following are a few symptoms you may be experiencing:

- As blood is directed to your muscles and brain, your digestion slows. You may be experiencing "butterflies" in your stomach.
- Your breathing gets faster. You may find it hard to catch your breath.
- Your heart rate goes up, along with your blood pressure.
- You find yourself waking up at 4:00 a.m., unable to go back to sleep.
- You feel irritable and get angry more easily, even with those who are nearest and dearest.

- You start to feel tense. Muscles feel tight. You may experience lower back problems.
- Your immune system is under attack. You are more susceptible to colds and flu.

If you are inclined to say, "So what?" read on. People who are suffering from a stress-related problem cause 75 percent of all visits to a doctor. Stress-related problems are also the greatest contributor to absenteeism.

A recent study published by the Canadian Heart and Stroke Foundation revealed that 43 percent of Canadians suffered from stress. That means that for every two people who are reading this book, one of you is likely suffering from stress. The numbers are staggering. The cause is also disturbing. This study listed the main causes as being related to home, family and work.

A US study revealed similar frightening results. In their book *Stress Management*, Dr. Edward Charlesworth and Dr. Ronald Natham listed the following statistics:

- 30 million Americans have some form of major heart or blood vessel disease.
- 1 million Americans have a heart attack every year.
- 25 million Americans have high blood pressure.
- 8 million Americans have ulcers.
- 12 million Americans are alcoholics.
- 5 billion doses of tranquilizers are prescribed each year.

It may surprise you to know that this study was conducted more than 15 years ago. You can imagine the current numbers. Using poetic license on an old song, we can safely say, "This is the dawning of the age of anxiety."

Nevertheless, it is actually easy to explain the cause of stress. Stress is defined by control. If you have control over a situation, your stress will go down. On the other hand, if you lose control, or lack control, your stress will go up. You may relate to the following example: Stress is being told you had the winning number in the lottery, when you can't find the ticket. Whether or not you find this example humorous, it's worth pointing out that many people start their workday wishing for some kind of "winning ticket," but most likely face more workplace challenges instead.

Many desire consistency and predictability in the workplace. Unfortunately, in the era of downsizing, restructuring and cutbacks, insecurity and unpredictability are part of our culture. Is it any wonder that our work environment greatly contributes to the stress in our lives, simply because it is even less predictable and supportive?

The solution lies in improving your level of communication. Most people will feel more in control if they understand the challenges and what is expected of them. Regardless of the stress the workplace throws at you, and believe us stress is unavoidable, you will be able to cope better if you have a clear understanding of the goals and expectations.

Understanding and Being Understood

Effective communication is a two-way process—summed up as *understanding and being understood.* More than a simple process of speaking and writing clearly, it is the ability to hear and understand accurately what another person has *intended* to communicate. It is also the ability to communicate intended messages successfully and to obtain feedback to ensure the messages were received accurately.

In any relationship people must communicate, and such communication is always subject to distortion and misunderstanding. Messages can be fact, feeling or a combination of fact and feeling. Consequently, effective communication implies understanding and being sensitive to many aspects of the communication process, such as assumptions, attitudes and values of persons communicating context and language. Unless the parties involved have the skill and the inclination to minimize miscommunication and to correct misunderstanding as it occurs, a positive relationship is not likely to develop or be maintained.

Effective communication exists between two people when the receiver interprets the sender's message in the same way the sender intended it.

How Important Is Listening?

The answer is, "very important." It is one of the most important communication skills to learn and do well. It is also the one communication skill about which we hear most complaints. Unfortunately, as stated by Beverly Kaye and Sharon Jordan-Evans in *Love'Em or Lose'Em: Getting Good People to Stay,* "Most managers don't really believe that listening is a critical skill. They believe that being results-oriented or customer-focused is much more important to business success than being a good listener."

Sometimes managers may believe they are good listeners when, in fact, they are not. They do not realize that listening is hard work. They treat listening as if it were a spectator sport. They sit back passively and hear what the person is saying, but they are not actively involved in the listening process.

Effective listening means being involved. It is active, not passive. It also does not mean simply hearing. Some people protest, "I'm a good listener; I can even repeat everything he said." The problem is that these managers make the incorrect assumption that the mere act of allowing the person to talk is equal to listening. They take listening skills for granted and often assume they are better at listening than they really are. They also assume that simply hearing and remembering means understanding.

Today's world of e-mail, voice-mail and face-to-face communication demands a great deal of our attention and energy. Many employers recognize the importance of good listening skills. They read the studies that show that employees are required to spend most of their time listening. These employers also realize that a great percentage of an employee's salary is paid to them for the skill of listening. They are also aware that employees listen at only an efficiency rating of 25 percent (we cover this in depth in the next section: *Is It So Hard for You to Listen?*). That means a lot of wasted money, and a negative effect on the bottom line due to misunderstood instructions.

It's interesting to note that traditionally in the world of sales, people were taught to speak more effectively and "go for the close." Nevertheless, studies indicate that salespeople who listen more than they talk, make more sales. Consequently, the current emphasis is on letting the customer talk while the salesperson listens. The focus has become, "First find out what they want, understand their needs and build a relationship." The same is true in the area of customer care. No wonder there has been a growing trend in the business community of sending employees to courses on listening skills.

The gift of active listening is priceless, because so few of us know how to give it.

Is It So Hard for You to Listen?

Have you ever been asked this question in an accusatory tone? If you have, we suggest you answer, "Yes it is!" When it comes to communication skills, listening is the hardest one of all. We have been teaching interpersonal communication skills for many years, and even though we pride ourselves on our ability in this area, there is still much room for improvement.

Why is it so hard to listen effectively? Dr. Ralph G. Nichols headed a national committee in the US devoted to research in effective listening, and found that we listen at a proficiency rating of only 25 percent—a figure we have mentioned before. His tests of comprehension show that without training, people are not very good at listening.

I suppose these results should not surprise us, simply because most of us have never received any training on how to listen. Think back to your school days and I'm sure you can remember lessons on reading and writing. You may even remember some attempts at teaching you to speak properly. But listening? Even working in the area, we don't recall ever taking a class about listening.

Most likely, the assumption in those days was that listening simply required paying attention and hearing what was said. Today, unfortunately, many people manifest a similar assumption.

Listening is a demanding process and requires extra energy. It demands concentration and tuning out distractions. It is an active process. It is also the one form of communication that we are required to use most often.

You may be surprised to know that a recent survey, described in the book *Interplay: The Process of Interpersonal Communication* by Ronald Adler, indicates that during the day we spend on average 53 percent of our time listening. The survey breaks down our communication activity as follows:

- writing, 14 percent;
- speaking, 16 percent;
- reading, 17 percent;
- face-to-face listening, 21 percent; and
- mass listening, 32 percent.

Clearly, not only does listening require more energy than any other form of communication, but it also demands the most of our time.

Besides our lack of training for such a demanding skill, another major problem is our limited attention span. We live in a talk-oriented society. We get inundated with all kinds of communication babble that is sometimes difficult to escape. Have you ever noticed how the volume of a television commercial seems louder than the program you're watching? Is it any wonder we learn to "tune out" in the midst of all that noise?

We are also used to being entertained. How often have you found it difficult to listen to a person who talked in a monotone manner, or whose voice did not sound pleasant? Maybe you found the subject matter boring so you escaped and let your mind wander to more pleasant thoughts. Perhaps you will admit that unless the speaker is interesting and can engage you with their style or topic, you just won't listen.

We have compiled some other reasons that make it difficult to improve your listening skills, along with some suggestions:

1. **I'm not interested.** Do you ever find yourself thinking, "This stuff he's talking about is really boring," or "I hope she's finished talking soon, so I can get back to what I was doing." If you answer "yes," you might as well accept that you are not listening. To improve your skill, simply search for something of interest to you in the conversation. Develop a frame of mind that is curious and know that no matter what the other person is talking about, there is always something worth understanding.

2. **I get tired when I'm listening.** We all do. Listening takes energy, more energy than talking. So do yourself a favor and exercise your mind. Develop your capacity to listen. When you work at getting yourself in physical shape, you increase the level of difficulty and, eventually, what used to be hard for you becomes easier. Improving your capacity to listen works in the same way. Every time you "raise the bar" and stick with it, you will improve. You will have more energy to listen.

3. **I get distracted.** Do you find yourself being easily distracted by the sounds around you, other people's conversations, the phone ringing or machinery operating? If that's the case, close your door or find a quiet place that allows you to focus on the other person.

4. **I can't get a word in.** How often do you jump in and offer your opinion, or start to talk about your agenda? If the answer is even, "just sometimes," then you're not listening. You cannot listen if you are talking. You are also not listening while you are preparing your response. This one is easy. Stop talking!

5. **I find myself thinking about other things.** Now this one is a major problem. Did you know that we are not really designed to be good listeners? We say this because most people talk at a speed of about 125 words per minute. Yet, we think at a much faster rate. Research shows that we can think at a rate four times faster than a person can speak. That means your mind can be thinking of about four words while the other person has only been able to say one. The answer, of course, is concentration. Focus on what is being said. Listen between the lines. Pay attention to the whole message, including the non-verbal communication.

Difficult as it is, listening skills can be improved. Better listening among co-workers will lead to greater understanding and a healthier workplace. HELP others listen to you!

You're Not Listening!

How often have you wanted to make the above statement to someone at work? Or have they perhaps said it to you? If your answer is, "too often," then please join the rest of us. This problem usually occurs when we are not paying as much attention to our listening habits as we are to other things. We sometimes engage in habits that annoy, and sometimes anger, the very people to whom we should be listening. Now in case you are saying, "I never do that!" see if you recognize any of the following habits.

The other person...
(a) interrupts me when I talk;
(b) never sits still;
(c) finishes my sentences for me;
(d) looks at the clock while I'm talking;
(e) looks out the window;
(f) glances at a note pad or computer screen;
(g) never looks at me while I'm talking;
(h) looks me in the eye but never smiles;
(i) smiles even when I'm talking about a serious problem;
(j) doodles and draws pictures while I'm talking;
(k) acts like listening to me is doing me a favor
(l) answers a question with another question;
(m) shows no expression to let me know if I'm being understood;
(n) frequently asks me to "get to the point";
(o) tries to get me off topic with irrelevant questions and comments.

Other non-listening observations:

_____

_____

_____

_____

_____

Put Yourself in My Place

When another person speaks, we are usually "listening" at one of four levels:

1.   We may be ignoring the other person, not really listening at all.
2.   We may be pretending to listen.
3.   We may be listening selectively, hearing only certain parts of the conversation.
4.   We may be paying attention and focusing on the words that are being said.

There is a fifth level—though very few of us ever practice this highest form of listening—*empathic listening.* Empathic listening is one of the best ways to truly understand another person. It is also a very important skill that, when used effectively, will strengthen your working relationships. When you practice empathy, your first goal is to understand, to experience their experience, to see and feel what the other person sees and feels. The meaning of the word "empathy" is actually derived from two Greek words that mean "feeling (in)side." The most common saying used to describe it is "to walk a mile in their shoes." When we say we are empathizing with someone, we are *experiencing* the other person's perception. You might say that you are temporarily seeing the world through their eyes.

On the cognitive level, empathy involves understanding a person from their perspective or point of view. It does not mean that you must accept their view. It simply means that you understand it. However, to fully understand them, cognition is not enough. Connecting only with your intellect, while not understanding the richness of a person's feelings, is no better than if you were a computer. You may be able to remember the words but you will not understand their true meaning.

Empathic listening involves using all your senses and skills to understand a person. You might be interested in knowing that in Chinese, the verb "to listen" is made up of the characters representing ears, eyes, undivided attention and heart.

Empathic listening is probably the most difficult form of interpersonal communication. As Stephen Covey writes in *The 7 Habits of Highly Effective People*, "Most people do not listen with the intent to understand; they listen with the intent to reply."

Most of us are just itching to get a word in ourselves. We get so caught up with our own agenda that we find it very difficult to suspend our judgments, and we fail to see things from the other's point of view. Sometimes, when we hear things that go against our own belief systems, we may block out the message or distort it to fit our reality. And, of course, there are those favorite "hot buttons" that trigger our emotions. A single word or phrase can stimulate a reaction within us that interferes with our ability to understand. (You can read more about the "hot button" concept in Chapter 6, Conflict.)

It is clear, if you really want to understand, and be understood, the answer lies in staying focused on the other person and suspending your own judgment. Forget about having the right answer. You do not have to agree with someone; however, you must fully and deeply understand that person, emotionally as well as intellectually. Empathic listening gets inside another person's frame of reference. You look out through it, and you see the world the way they see the world, and you understand how they feel. **The essence of empathic listening involves understanding each other on an emotional level.**

Empathic listening involves much more than registering, reflecting, or even understanding the words. In empathic listening you listen with your ears, and more important, you listen with your eyes and with your heart. You listen for feeling and meaning.

As you learn to listen deeply to other people, you will discover tremendous differences in perception. You will also begin to appreciate the impact these differences can have as people try to work together.

Empathy leads to understanding and being understood.

I See and I Understand

What you *do* can have more impact on your communication then what you *say*. According to UCLA's Dr. Albert Mehrabian, a researcher in the field of non-verbal behavior, your communication effectiveness depends on three critical factors:

Verbal: the message itself, the words you say;
Vocal: the tone, variety, projection and resonance of your voice;
Visual: what people see, specifically in your body language.

His research also revealed that *visual,* especially during the initial stages of a meeting, is the most influential factor. Body language has more of an impact than the tone, variety and projection of your voice and the actual words you use. You can believe that old saying, "a picture is worth a thousand words." Research has confirmed that thinking. Workshop participants will often ask us if that means that what they say is not important. Our tongue-in-cheek reply is usually, "Politicians have known about this for years. Forget content. As long as they look and sound good, people will vote for them."

To prove the importance of non-verbal and visual impressions, try a little experiment with a colleague: Sit facing the other person, look them in the eye and say, "I agree." However, as you say the words, frown and shake your head from side to side as if you are signaling "no." If that doesn't confuse them, we don't know what will.

It seems that we place greater belief in what we see than what we hear or what is said. If you have had the experience of talking to a person who is not familiar with your language, you know that a lot can be interpreted from non-verbal messages. We often make assumptions about a person's friendliness and how approachable they are by the way they look. So remember, even though you're not saying anything, you're still communicating. The saying that it's impossible *not* to communicate, is true.

If you want to create an environment that will make good communication easier, we suggest you use the S.O.F.T.E.N. approach. This approach, using non-verbal cues, will contribute to making discussions more satisfying, perhaps even enjoyable. The S.O.F.T.E.N. approach consists of the following six key behaviors:

Smile: As a first impression, an appropriate smile creates a pleasant tone. It lets people know that this is going to be a good discussion.

Open posture: Use your body language to show that you are willing to listen and that you are open to new ideas.

Forward lean: A slight lean towards the person gives the impression that you are interested and paying attention.

Touch: A good firm handshake (not a vice-grip or limp fish) is a good way to physically connect.

Eye contact: Face the person and gently look them in the eye (not a staring contest). You are showing that you want to get the full message.

Nodding: The occasional nod gives the message that you are listening and that you understand what is being said.

The fact that our visual presentation is of great importance does not mean we can forget about our vocal and verbal skills. It is still important that you make an effort to communicate with words as well. Words are still the best way to communicate your thoughts and ideas, while non-verbal communication is one of the best ways to express your feelings and attitude. Unfortunately, some non-verbal behavior can be misunderstood.

The most effective way to get your message across as clearly as possible is to combine the content of your message with a corresponding non-verbal message. This kind of communication is called *congruent sending*. When the content and the feeling you show are both the same, there is less chance of being misunderstood.

Just remember the power of your facial expressions, gestures, voice tone or other non-verbal messages. Do not try to hide your feelings, since a lack of visual cues will make interpretation more difficult. These signals represent a major resource in your ability to be understood. Combine these signals with the corresponding and appropriate words, and you increase the power and effectiveness of your communications.

Congruent sending as a communication skill is very useful when you want to solve a problem or resolve a conflict.

Some Helpful Hints

We're all familiar with the saying, "You never have a second chance to make a good first impression." Valuable and often lasting impressions are made within the first few minutes, even seconds, of contact with people. Your best efforts at communication may be wasted if you do not concentrate on creating a positive communication climate. Your tone of voice, your expression, your apparent receptiveness to the responses of others, all have tremendous impact on the success or failure of the communication process. Here are some helpful hints to practice in order to create a positive first impression:

- Tune people in and the world out;
- Put them at ease and make them feel important;
- Get them talking about themselves;
- Be sensitive and ask non-threatening questions;
- Hold eye contact and listen to how they feel.

The important message is to immediately set up a communication process where they talk and you listen. People will be more responsive to you if you take their interests and needs into account.

How People Make Meaning

By now you understand how difficult it can be to understand and be understood. We have described how *active listening, non-verbal communication* and *congruent sending* will greatly improve your chances of making this happen. Another factor that needs to be considered, is popularly known by the name Neuro-Linguistic Programming or NLP.

NLP was made famous by Grinder, Bandler, Cameron-Bandler and DeLozier. Since we will only present our personal understanding of the NLP techniques in very limited detail here, do visit your local bookstore or library if you want to find out more. There are many books available on this subject.

Two of the original books written on the subject were *Frogs into Princes* by Richard Bandler and John Grinder, and *Practical Magic* by Steve Lankton. Basically, they support the idea that we human beings transmit and receive messages through three primary representational systems. They are visual (see), auditory (hear) and kinesthetic (feel). We use these three systems to process information and understand our world. But it is important to note that each of us has what is called a "lead" system through which we represent or take in our experiences. This results in us having differences in what is called "digital presentation." The following are examples of how these presentations will differ according to a person's representational system.

- **Visual**: "This looks really good and clear to me." "I see what you are saying."
- **Auditory:** "Tell me in more detail what you are saying at this point in time." "This sounds really good to me."
- **Kinesthetic:** "This feels really good to me." "I feel really good about what we are doing."

These differences are not usually a problem when we are relaxed. Although we may have a primary representational system, we usually understand a person who is using words typical of one of the other systems. The problems start when we are stressed and feeling anxious. When we start to experience pressure, we flip to our primary system and we have difficulty comprehending the others. It is as if the pressure we experience causes the computer in our brain to function with only one program and to lock out the others. Let us illustrate.

Luke thought he knew all about these concepts and he considered himself a pretty good communicator during the first years of his relationship with his wife Susan. One fateful day, on his way to a meeting, he learned the truth about his abilities. He was driving, with Susan in the passenger seat, from Toronto to Ottawa. During a very pleasant drive, they shared their hopes and dreams, and talked about their future. The time seemed to have flown by as they entered the city limits more than four hours later.

That's when it started to happen. The meeting Luke was on his way to attend was important to him and he was feeling somewhat anxious to get there on time. Because he was unfamiliar with the city, he asked Susan to take the map from the glovebox and help him look for the location. Before you start thinking, "That was his first mistake," we want to point out that the ability to interpret a map is not the exclusive domain of men. However, Susan does admit that she has difficulty making sense of "those darn maps." This was something Luke was to become aware of in short order.

Soon they were both experiencing some stress—Susan, because she was trying to find a street that she couldn't seem to locate on the map, and Luke, because he was starting to think he might be late. He was also in the middle of some heavy traffic and was focused on getting there safely. As he tried to relax, he explained to Susan what to look for. The organizer of the meeting had given some directions. From these, Luke described a short dead-end side street she should see before they got to the area.

As you may have guessed, they passed by this small street without a sound or any indication from Susan. She simply looked confused. Before he realized it, they were on a one-way street, stuck in traffic, with no hope of getting to his meeting on time. What ensued was a major fight, where both of them insisted they were right. Luke was adamant that he had been very clear with his instructions, while Susan was equally as adamant, saying that his instructions were anything *but* clear.

Reviewing this example, you can now appreciate why two people who normally communicate quite well can suddenly have difficulty understanding one another. In Susan and Luke's case, the problem arose when they both experienced stress. She started to feel stressed when she was asked to interpret the map, so she accessed her primary system (**auditory**). Luke was also feeling stressed as his concern grew about not getting to the meeting, so he accessed his primary system (**visual**). So here he was telling her to "see this," "look for that," and "you'll see it clearly marked." Susan, on the other hand, was confused because nothing "sounded right," nor was he giving her "the details or the right words."

This experience was one of the first to teach Luke the value of not trying to communicate when you are upset or stressed. He had been told that overstimulation and understimulation are the twin evils of inefficient listening. By his own admission, his problem doesn't seem to be understimulation. He just has to remind himself occasionally not to get so excited, and to take a deep breath.

The message is clear. The worst climate for effective interpersonal communication is one where both parties are feeling defensive, angry or stressed. The best climate is when both parties are concerned for each other, have high self-esteem and are relaxed.

Twelve Steps to Better Communication

Practicing the following 12 steps will help you to achieve a better working relationship through better communication.

1. **Stop talking.** The first step to better communication is to keep quiet while another person speaks.
2. **Put the speaker at ease.** Use the S.O.F.T.E.N. approach. Help the speaker feel free to talk to you by creating a supportive communication climate.
3. **Empathize.** Put yourself in the other person's place. As might be said in a visual way, "look through another person's lens and see a different world."
4. **Show that you want to listen.** Stop what you're doing. Demonstrate that you are interested and that you want to understand.
5. **Remember your thinking speed.** Use your thinking speed wisely. Focus your attention on the words, ideas and feelings of the person. Use the "extra" time to summarize what they have been saying.
6. **Get rid of distractions.** Choose a quiet place where you won't be disturbed. Don't fidget, play with your pen, doodle or shuffle papers. Tune in to the person.
7. **Don't give up too soon.** Wait until the speaker is finished and has expressed a complete thought. "Patience is a virtue."
8. **Share the burden.** Good communication is a partnership. It is understanding and being understood. It demands energy and skills from both individuals.
9. **Keep your cool.** Control your anger. When you are angry, you are focused on your own feelings and not the speaker's.
10. **Ask questions.** Make sure you are understanding and receiving the speaker's thoughts and feelings accurately. Get clarification by asking questions.

11. **Avoid being critical.** Criticism puts the speaker on the defensive. Make it a win-win situation.
12. **Practice, practice and practice.** Make a commitment to improve your communication skills and keep practicing until it becomes a habit.

Joe Sherren's "The Birds"©

Effective communication begins with the act of giving part of yourself to the other person.

Over the years we have observed many things about the differences in the way people communicate. We have attended numerous seminars, read many books, conducted informal studies, and have even become certified to teach models on behavioral science.

The resources were all designed to improve our understanding of each other's personalities and attitudes. But many of them often miss the most important point. The point being, how can we quickly identify and adapt our communication for a wide range of diverse individuals, in order to be more effective in achieving mutual goals?

Joe Sherren has spent the last 15 years developing a model that he has used successfully to help people create powerful communication connections. We are presenting it in this book in the hope that it will help you develop skills in how to quickly identify, through a variety of signals, what another person requires from you when you are sending messages. Of course, the information is also intended to help you understand how to modify your style to one most suitable for the individuals you are trying to motivate, influence or change.

This document has been used as a supplementary take-away for participants who have attended our high-impact, interactive seminar "Creating Communication Connections." Those who participate are able to experience a series of scenarios, which in turn help them discover the primary strengths and weaknesses of how they communicate and interact with people of similar and different communication styles.

As many of us realize, the field of behavioral communications is not an exact science. Although there are those who will look for specific answers and an exact formula for developing better relationships, there are none. What we have been able to do, by utilizing many attitudinal studies and personality models developed over the last 40 years, is to create a model that will give practitioners a higher probability of success in their communication effectiveness.

To make the concept simpler, easier to follow and more efficient to relate, we have assigned each of the communication styles the name of a bird. The attributes of the bird closely relate to the communication style of the individuals who fall into that group. The four communication styles are:

- Eagle
- Dove
- Peacock
- Owl

Everyone will have a one, two, three, four communication-style sequence. For example, one would be your primary style, two your secondary style and so on, with the fourth style being your weakest. Most people will have a strong primary style and secondary style. Others may also have a third style which might strongly influence the other two. We will outline the fundamental strengths and weaknesses of each of the styles as well as the more finite differences, depending on the order of the other influencing styles.

What follows is a communication analysis. Please circle the letter beside the statement, which reflects your number one choice in answer to each question.

A Communication Analysis

1. **What is your preferred way of dressing?**
   - (E) Designer, classy, more formal
   - (P) Bold colors, trendy, informal, lots of black
   - (D) Gentle muted colors, casual, loose sweaters, track suits
   - (O) Conservative, classic, practical, businesslike

2. **In meetings, are you more?**
   - (E) Direct and to the point
   - (P) Animated, excitable, friendly
   - (D) Dreamy thoughts, peacemaker, casual
   - (O) Specific, concise, accurate

3. **Which of the following would be your preferred shape?**

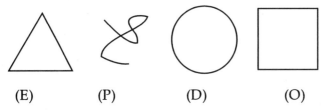

   (E)   (P)   (D)   (O)

4. **When making critical decisions, you require?**
   - (E) Options for various courses of action
   - (P) Testimonials from trusted others
   - (D) Assurances and support
   - (O) Evidence and proof

5. **If given free choice, where would you most prefer to live?**
   - (E) Suburban palace, 2-story, 4-bedroom, paved driveway
   - (P) Country home on acreage with friendly neighbors
   - (D) Cabin in the woods with peace and tranquility
   - (O) Condo or townhouse in a downtown area, eat out a lot

6. *Your most favored vacation would be?*
   (E) Adventures and travel
   (P) Caribbean resort—sun, sand, lounging
   (D) At home or at a cottage—rest, reading and friends
   (O) Organized city or country tour

7. *When attending a seminar, you would prefer?*
   (E) Practical information that is brief and summarized, few workshops
   (P) Lots of fun learning, jokes, analogies
   (D) Comfortable, low-pressure environment, no role playing, nice people
   (O) Logically laid out, not ambiguous information, follow the agenda

8. *Which of the following motivates you more than the others?*
   (E) Getting and seeing results
   (P) Recognition and applause
   (D) Personal attention and friendship
   (O) Lots of organized activity going on

9. *Is your office more?*
   (E) Neat and organized
   (P) Disorganized with fun stuff, files in piles
   (D) Friendly with comfortable chairs and personal pictures
   (O) Working environment, laid out practical, wall board

10. *Your preferred way to sleep?*
    (E) On your back, straight out
    (P) In a cuddling or almost fetal position
    (D) On your side with your knees slightly bent
    (O) On your stomach with your arms up by your head

11. *Are you more?*

(E) High-assertive and reserved

(P) High-assertive and outgoing

(D) Less-assertive and outgoing

(O) Less-assertive and reserved

12. *An appropriate summary of your strengths, not the role you play in your profession, would be?*

(E) Getting to the bottom line of complex problems, and making critical decisions.

(P) Seeing the bigger picture, conceptualizing, using your intuition and being creative.

(D) Interpersonal relationships, helping others get along, expressing feelings as comfortably as ideas, working in teams.

(O) Establishing standards, maintaining self-discipline, admiring others who maintain a sense of discipline and quality about their work.

What this survey is designed to do is determine your primary and your secondary strengths in the area of communication. In this test, the letters are represented as follows:

(E)	=	Eagle	Quantity	_____
(D)	=	Dove	Quantity	_____
(P)	=	Peacock	Quantity	_____
(O)	=	Owl	Quantity	_____

Count up the scores in each of the letters and order from the highest to the lowest. This will give you an indication of your preferred way of communicating.

Birds of a Feather

These birds have certain characteristics and behaviors, which we associate with them. We find that in the communication process, people also exhibit similar characteristics—and we can relate them to each of these birds. In short, the people to whom we assign each of the styles appear to share similar characteristics with the respective birds.

Just as bird watchers delight in watching birds and their behaviors, you will enjoy watching for these "birds" among your friends, family and professional aquaintances.

The Eagle

Eagles can be quickly recognized by their very serious, concentrated and stern look when you are communicating with them. They can stare at you for long periods of time without blinking. They normally have short, neat hair. Their clothes are quite tidy and tucked in and, even in casual situations, will have a professional flair to them.

When answering the phone they will just say things like "Bill here," or "This is Sam." If they are in charge, even their answering machines are quick and to the point. When they leave messages for others they will just say "This is Bill, call me."

Generally, Eagles like their information presented to them in a bottom-line and netted-out fashion. When speaking with them be brief and direct, stick to business, and assure them that results will be achieved. Focus on what you want and how you want it.

Strengths associated with Eagles are their ability to make decisions, even critical ones, quite quickly. They can adapt quickly to change and like to take on new challenges. They feel there is no obstacle that can't be overcome and they are usually optimistic about the future.

Eagles do have some weaknesses. They will often put results

ahead of other people's feelings. They seem to always be in a hurry, they are not very patient and will cut you off, if you do not get to the point very quickly. They will often give you an answer, before you have finished asking your question.

Sometimes, they appear to push people around, are regarded as poor listeners, and certainly do not like working in teams unless they are in charge. Do not expect them to express personal feelings if you do not know them well. They might become preoccupied with other matters if you start rambling on during a conversation.

When we ask them to choose between four shapes—circle, triangle, squiggle or square—the Eagle will select the triangle. It has been said that people who choose the triangle first, tend to be pre-occupied with sexual thoughts and see themselves as being great lovers. This is a pointed wedge shape, which can push further and release greater energy than any other form.

In a study at the Yale University Child Development Clinic, it was observed that the triangle symbol required a more developed connection between the brain and hand. The normal child did not draw this form until the age of five, though the circle and square were accomplished at three and four years of age.

Children who are Eagles tend to be aggressive and energetic. In drawings they might depict steeples, airplanes and sailboats. Their doodling would have many pointy figures in them. Even their handwriting will be hard on the paper with strong points in it.

Experiments at Yale University and at McGill University in Montreal have indicated that emotions are affected by the action in the hypothalamus in the center of the brain. By electrically stimulating this portion of the brain, responses of love, hate, fear, aggressiveness and sex have been evoked.

Aggressiveness is closely identified with the sex urge, since they both produce a high degree of excitation and seek active outlets for this energy. So, as children or adults, if these people are not able to satisfy one of these urges, they will replace it with another.

Sigmund Freud makes reference to the triangle as being a phallic symbol, representing the sexual organs of the male and female. It has been said that the sexual instinct is the most powerful motivator. If this energy is not released, however, it can also cause unhealthy behaviors.

Eagles are sharp thinkers and have keen perception. They will arrive at solutions quickly. Independent thinkers, they resist being placed in any position subordinate to others. They have the ability to work independently and that's what they enjoy.

Eagles can be emotional, but are not sensitive or compassionate to the emotional needs of others. They are direct, and like to get to the point quickly. Most people like and admire Eagles from a distance, but are apprehensive about approaching them on an intimate basis.

When communicating with Eagles, be brief and direct, they want you to get to the point with no frills. Focus on what you want, and let them have control. Do not waste their time with details because they grasp broad concepts quickly and will quickly turn off.

Eagles like to learn by trying out ideas, theories and techniques to see if they work in practice. Consequently, they visualize new ideas and look for opportunities to try them.

For example, they often return from a conference or workshop excited about new ideas and eager to take some related action right away. Eagles like to get on with things and tend to act quickly and confidently on any idea which captures their interest.

They tend to be impatient with touchy-feely discussions, and any talk that does not come to a fast conclusion. They are practical, down-to-earth people who like making fast decisions and solving complex problems.

Eagles see problems and opportunities as a challenge. Their philosophy is: "There is always a better way," and "If it works, that's what matters."

When sleeping, Eagles like to be on their back, straight out, and they take up lots of space. They prefer to live in the typical suburban palace, two-story four-bedroom house with a circular driveway. To please them, it should have a formal dining area, paved driveway with a fancy car and lawn sprinklers. When entertaining they are likely to plan the event well in advance to ensure that it goes smoothly. They like it to be professional and organized and would prefer on the patio—garden-style with a tablecloth and wine—or in a formal dining room with silver.

For vacations, Eagles prefer adventure and action. Whether it is camping in the wilderness, hiking, fishing, skiing, golf, or even white water rafting, they like to be active and not sit around. To them it is a waste of a vacation to do nothing.

Their office is often neat and organized, with their qualifications, trophies and certificates of achievement on display. If possible, they have their large power furniture arranged in an "I'm in charge here" layout.

As we noted, everyone has both a primary and secondary style of receiving communication. If we can recognize and remember this idea, we could possibly increase our effectiveness by as much as 75 percent. Following is a list of the combined, Eagle-dominant styles.

Eagle-Doves

Eagle-Dove combinations are self-motivated individuals with an inexhaustible supply of energy, which constantly needs to be released. People are important to someone exhibiting this combination. Their need to give love is greater than their need to receive it. In associations with others they become the giver rather than the taker.

Eagle-Doves want to take action quickly and will not wait around for somebody else to make a move or to come up with an idea. They enjoy competition and challenges and they do not discourage easily.

Eagle-Doves have quick minds and frequently act on impulse and intuition. Projects that tend to go on for a long time begin to bore the Eagle in them because they constantly like new challenges.

Sometimes they can be understanding and compassionate, but that trait is often overruled by their impatient urge to get on with the job. One problem with this combination is that they develop internal stress from their conflicting impulses. On one hand, they are sensitive to the feelings of others. On the other hand, they just want to get on with it and will walk over people to get to where they want to go. Then, because of the Dove influence, they will feel badly about what they have done.

Individuals with the Eagle-Dove combination, with a strong Peacock influence, are highly energetic and are more imaginative. They will come up with creative approaches to achieve what they are determined to accomplish.

They will become easily upset by others who do not treat them fairly, and will lose their temper quickly. However, they will just as quickly forgive, and carry on as if nothing has happened.

Eagle-Owls

Eagle-Owl individuals are more left-brain than other combinations. They are not into self-appreciation, and that quality also makes them a much easier person to live with than some of the other types. Their aggressive energy looks for constructive outlets that depend more upon their skills and abilities, than being emotionally fed by others.

They are able to evaluate a situation quickly, using reason and logic and make the decisions necessary to resolve it. Normally, they do not allow emotions to interfere with reason. They are realistic, with both feet on the ground, and do not waste time fantasizing or daydreaming.

Eagle-Owl combinations with Dove dominance are able to experience more creative thought. They will occasionally find the time to look for romance and idealism in the things they do.

Eagle-Peacocks

With Eagle-Peacocks, you must get to the facts very quickly and not waste time when communicating with them. For best results, you must immediately become very personable. It would be wise to show them that you also appreciate fun in life and even fit a joke into the conversation.

They are highly independent and individualistic people. They have great power of imagination and possess high aggressive energy that gives them unlimited scope for expression. They generate great amounts of mental activity, which require creative outlets.

They will not be controlled by conventionalism, tradition or socially acceptable norms. Even though they like to be in the company of others, they find they must be in control and are most productive and creative when in seclusion. They can be stimulated both by facts and imagination and will use this combination to artistically express themselves.

Eagle-Peacocks have a great desire to leave their mark on the universe and contribute to improving society in some way. However, they also want the recognition for doing it before they die.

If these people have a dominant Owl trait, they are more conscious of a need to feel secure in actual living situations. Because of the combination, they conform and live by the rules of the society more easily.

If their dominant third style is Dove, they will want to be very sensitive to others, but at the same time, will not let anyone get in the way of them achieving their goals. They have a need to connect and be close to others, but usually end up with only a few close friends.

The Peacock

Peacocks can be recognized by their bright clothes and big, friendly grin. They usually have a twinkle in their eyes that makes people wonder what they are up to, or what mischievous thoughts they are having. While some people have a "bad hair day," Peacocks have a "bad hair" life. No matter what they do, they seem never to be satisfied with how their hair turns out.

When answering the phone their voice and words are optimistic and cheerful. When you ask how they are, they will always answer "great," "wonderful" or "sensational," or provide some other lively response. They will usually sound truly pleased to talk to you.

People with great imaginations, they can be very creative, and behave optimistically in most situations. They get along fabulously with people, and have a charisma that attracts others to them instantly. They are never at a loss for words in a social situation.

In their natural state, they are outgoing, spontaneous and highly expressive. You can recognize them by their clothes because they usually go for bright and fancy colors, but they also have strong leaning towards wearing black. Although they are very enthusiastic, they will react quickly to any perceived threat. Their main mission is to enjoy life.

On the negative side, they will interrupt when you are speaking, tend to exaggerate, and if they listen at all, it is only to see when you are going to stop talking so they know when to start. They are poor time managers and often arrive at meetings late. They like new projects but become bored quickly and go looking for something else. They do not like detailed work and may not follow through on important items, which causes them problems with their work.

The symbol that tends to attract them first is the squiggle. This is even apparent in their handwriting, which is usually hard to read, and does not always stay on the line. The squiggle is the symbol of imagination and creativity. This is one of their dominant characteristics and they bring their creativity and open mindedness to all aspects of their lives. While many of their ideas could never be implemented, they are fascinating to hear and to debate.

Their imagination is stimulated by an intense desire to see and know more. They do not generally accept the status quo, and like to go off on adventures in search of new discoveries.

Sometimes they are not in touch with reality. Much of their thinking time is spent in higher thought, beyond the boring existence of everyday living.

They can be aggressive, especially if they have a strong Eagle presence. When their natural ability to be imaginative is suppressed, there will probably be negative consequences for the person who gets in their way. Peacocks must channel their energy into constructive activity. If this does not happen, they may become withdrawn or aggressive. They seem to be always searching for excitement and to others may not always appear to have two feet firmly on the ground.

When communicating with Peacocks, make it fun and stimulating and remember to smile. Use analogies for description—and place them as the most important person in the interaction; they thrive on public recognition. If you are trying to sell them on an idea or concept, arrange it so they will be recognized for their great insights and perception. Allow them to verbalize their ideas and visions.

In the learning process, Peacocks involve themselves fully and without reservation in new experiences. They enjoy the here and now and are happy to be dominated by immediate experiences. They are open-minded, not skeptical, and this tends to make them enthusiastic about anything new. Their philosophy is: "I'll try anything once." They tend to act first and consider the consequences later. Their days are filled with thought and activity.

Peacocks will tackle problems by brainstorming. As soon as the excitement from one activity has died down, they are busy looking for the next. They thrive on the challenge of new experiences, but are bored with implementation and maintaining over the longer-term consolidation. They are gregarious people, constantly involving themselves with others, but in doing so, always put themselves at the center of all activity.

Peacocks prefer to sleep in the more fetal position. Whether their sleep mates be people, pillows or pets, they like to cuddle. They would prefer living in a country home on an acreage, perhaps have horses or other animals, and spend their leisure time visiting and joking with friendly neighbors.

For vacations, they like to get away to a Caribbean beach resort. They love to spend most of their time in the sun, resting, relaxing and talking to people at the swim-up pool bar.

Their offices are usually cluttered. They will have toys and cartoons. Much of the time they will have files sitting around in piles. Once in awhile they will make an effort to clean it up, but to no avail. In the end, it just returns to the way it was.

Peacock-Doves

The Peacock-Dove combination is sensitive and idealistic, looking for beauty and romance at every opportunity. They search for an ideal love that will go beyond the normal relationship. They can often be found alone in thought. They like the warmth and security of being with people. The greatest pleasure they experience is their love for other human beings.

Friends are often a disappointment as they seldom live up to the ideal image Peacock-Doves have of people. They become disappointed in the relationships. They can be warm and responsive to people who accept them as an individual and who recognize the creative person they are. Although sensitive and idealistic, when threatened by an outside force or person, they can become aggressive. They will defend a principle to the end, even if their security is in danger.

Peacock-Owls

When communicating with Peacock-Owls, make sure that, after your initial friendliness, you follow up with accurate and appropriate facts and details. These people are both dreamy and realistic at the same time. They will mentally wander into their imaginations, then wake up to the safer practicalities of the real world. Their openness to new ideas and willingness to see and accept change can work positively in developing an inherent ability to adjust to change.

Since their need for security is also very strong, they try to keep both feet on the ground consistently enough to function as a member of the social environment. Home may be important, but variety and change are needed to keep them excited. If strong Eagle tendencies are present, they could become hostile and foster resentment, especially when they are interrupted or held back.

They are more involved with themselves than with other people. Personal relationships might take a backseat to other interests. Even family is more a means of securing their need for home stability, than for exchanging personal love. They are not easily influenced by other people or emotional attachments.

Peacock-Eagles

Peacock-Eagles are dynamic individuals who possess all the qualities for success and leadership. Their mind is never at rest, and they can never seem to stop thinking and planning. They take laptop computers on vacation, because their minds are in high gear all the time.

They have an ability to conceptualize and bring abstract ideas into focus with accurate comprehension. Their ability to do it usually results in solid theories. They can absorb knowledge and understand abstract concepts without working at it too hard. However, they expect others to follow through with details of their projects, because they become bored with follow-up and detailed procedures.

These people are great at being able to conceptualize, create and develop solutions. However, do not expect them to be around when it comes to actually implanting the solutions.

Challenges are a source of stimulation and pleasure. They search for a variety of areas where they can discharge their mental energies, which are continuously building up as they are being released. Although receptive to new ideas, they will not be led down the garden path by ideas that do not conform to some sort of intelligent order.

In relationships, these people are either envied or idolized. Unfortunately, they do not make the ideal companion or mate, because they spend little time developing interpersonal relationships and are quite intolerant of the weaknesses of others. They have a strong need for companionship, consciously or unconsciously finding relationships with people who have similar values. Security is not a strong motivator for these people, and they are unable to truly relax and enjoy the company of others.

Those with a strong Owl influence are even less motivated to develop strong relationships and have little compassion and patience with others. They do not suffer fools gladly.

They will resist social situations and shy away from being part of a group. Very little of their free time is devoted to parties or play, and even humor must be sprinkled with provocative thought to be appealing.

The Dove

Doves can be spotted by their sincere, friendly smile, their warm eyes, their loose, untucked clothing and relaxed posture. They will have a relaxed handshake, and they will buy shoes for comfort rather than style. The symbol they are most often drawn to is the circle, which is the symbol of peace, love and harmony. Doves are very much into tranquility and pursue it in all areas of their lives.

Their handwriting tends to be rounded with emphasis being on a circular motion as well as curls at the end of words. To understand why the circle is referred to as the symbol of love, think of pleasure items that are round, soft and warm. For a child, it is a rattle, a ball, and a mother's warm breasts, which are a comfort and delight. Doves prefer objects with no sharp edges to hurt them. They respond to round smooth objects, which soothe, pacify and provide safe play.

The preference is reflected in a Dove's behavior. They do not like violence, will run away from a fight, shrink at the sight of an accident, and find tense arguments distressing. What Doves seek mostly is affection and approval, which they find in non-threatening situations. They tend not to be hostile or aggressive and would rather play than fight. Doves do have a tendency to be possessive and jealous about people who are close to them, as well as items that bring them personal pleasure.

When communicating with a Dove, you must be sincere in your approach, agreeable and supportive. You must not come on too strong or in a panic. Focus on what you want and how you want it. Be patient with them and give them time to adjust their thinking, to allow them to respond appropriately. If you can make a personal connection with someone they know and trust, they will more likely listen to you and absorb what you are saying.

Their voice mail usually says something like "Good morning, this is Sally, I'm sorry I am not here to take you call. Your call is very important to me. Please leave your name and number and I will be sure to get back to you as soon as I can."

When learning, Doves like to stand back to ponder experiences and observe from many different perspectives. They collect data, both first-hand and from others, and prefer to think about it thoroughly before coming to any conclusion. They tend to postpone reaching and announcing definitive conclusions for as long as possible.

Their operating philosophy is to be cautious. Doves are thoughtful people who like to consider all possible angles and implications before making a move. They prefer to take a back seat in meetings and discussions. They enjoy observing other people in action. They listen to others and get the drift of the discussion before making their own points. Doves tend to adopt a low profile and have a quiet, tolerant, relaxed air about them. When they react, they consider the whole picture, which includes the sum total of all their experiences and observations.

Other characteristics of Doves include their tendency to sleep on their sides in the spoon position—and the fact that they would prefer the tranquility of living in a cabin in the woods and enjoying their solitude to city living. They enjoy being independent, watching sunsets, relaxing, floating around in a paddleboat, and having their family and close friends accessible when necessary.

They often prefer a vacation at someone's home or cottage where they can sleep in, catch up on their reading, see some friends and visit family. At work, even their office has a friendly atmosphere to it, decorated with pictures and comfortable chairs. When co-workers come to them for favors, they have a hard time saying "no," and people often take advantage of them. Other people sometimes see their friendly and accommodating nature as a weakness and will try to exploit that loyalty.

Doves are warm and friendly people who listen actively and are very patient. They value personal relationships above all and can be articulate, organized and work cohesively with others. They really like to work in areas and with others who get along. You can always count on a Dove, when they give you their word. They have good counseling skills and are usually known around the office as peacemakers, because they like to help others.

In meetings Doves do not always push for what they want. When making a decision they solicit input from as many people they can. They often know what the decision is going to be, but input from others helps confirm what they already know.

When you first meet a Dove, you should not come on too strong. The behavior will remind them of a used-car salesman and they will back off. They are very trusting, get let down by people and worry too much about what others think.

They do not like change that people have not had time to get used to and accept. They spend too much personal time doing things for others. Doves avoid taking risks and avoid conflict at all costs. They wait too long to act, and will hold a grudge against anyone who has done them wrong in the past.

Dove-Owls

Dove-Owls who have Eagle dominance are highly motivated by love and the desire to share that love. They will then try to secure that love by creating an infrastructure of family, home and a circle of friends. They will guard against any outside threat that might disturb the lifestyle they have put together. Their strong desire for love often manifests itself in their quest for achievement and a strong sexual drive. Because of the opposing nature of these styles (Dove-Eagle), these individuals may cause themselves internal stress in their relationships with other people.

Those with Peacock dominance are very similar, except they combine all this with lofty visions of great accomplishments. Although the need for security is highest in their motivation, they first must achieve a loving, secure relationship. Normally, they do not focus on completing pragmatic goals, other than creating a comfortable family home. They tend to avoid fights and do their best to stay away from situations involving conflict. Their large capacity for pleasure, combined with their creative nature, causes them to go out of their way trying to bring happiness to lots of people.

Dove-Peacocks

Dove-Peacocks with strong Owl attributes have two extremes to their nature. One is taking the time to be playful, compassionate and enjoying the pleasure of being with people. The other is an aggressive drive to get ahead without interference of feelings that might slow them down. Unfortunately, the two extremes could ultimately come together and serve to conceal their inner feelings. Many are realists with both feet on the ground. They prefer to accept and move on solid and sound ideas, rather than reach for the unreachable.

Dove-Peacocks with Owl strengths are romantic idealists. They search for a profound love with another individual to satisfy their every emotion and desire. They are extremely imaginative and will unconsciously invent an unreal image of others. The quality opens them up to possible disillusions and disappointments.

Wealth and social success are of less concern that other values, since they are interested in attaining loftier goals to satisfy their needs. To be a success in an artistic endeavor, they must have someone they can trust to represent them and protect them in the world.

Dove-Peacocks who have the spirit of an Eagle are more aggressive in their search for romance and more ambitious in finding outlets for their creative abilities. They will also stand up to other people who threaten their ideals and principles, and will fight for the principle of personal rights.

Dove-Eagles

Dove-Eagles with Peacock tendencies are motivated by the desire for love, which is also a major factor behind their sexual motivation and drive for success. They might have a touch of romanticism and frequent fantasies.

They are not concerned with financial security. These people are not afraid to face problems, and will focus on resolving them. Freedom always comes before safety. The best security for them is the freedom to express their feelings and abilities.

Often they will experience internal stress because their Dove traits will cause them to be sensitive to others. However, when the Eagle nature in them takes over, they will walk over anyone who gets in their way. Then, as a Dove, they will feel really bad because they hurt someone else's feelings. At times, as they think about it, they will not like themselves.

The Owl

Owls can be recognized by their cross-looking demeanor. In fact many will experience people coming up to them saying, "Are you angry at me for some reason? Have I done something to offend you?"

Even as children, Owls will often pout if things are not going their way. Their hair and clothes are practical, and they normally check the weather or the day's agenda before getting dressed.

You will find that many Owls have trouble looking at you directly in the eye and holding it for a period of time without blinking. As children, a higher proportion of them wear glasses.

Their voice mails usually will say a variation on "Good morning, this is Tuesday, May the second. I will be out of my office attending meetings until 11:00 a.m. I, then, plan to...*and so on*. Please leave your name, number, time of your call and the reason, *blah, blah*."

Their primary symbol choice is the square, which reflects a strong desire for security. For confirmation, look at how often the square-ness appears in their handwriting. This shape came into their lives the first time they were placed in a crib as an infant. It kept them safe and secure. Later, a playpen that was larger, but still square, pro-tected them from harm. They liked to play with blocks, and as their intelligence developed, they placed one on top of the other, building structures.

Because of their focus on security, their home is their castle. Whether it is gardening, taking care of repairs and improvements, entertaining in the home or generally puttering around, they are comfortable and content in a home situation. They like working with their hands and like to build things. Their gift of patience helps them follow through each step of a project until it's completed with accuracy. When this is carried to an extreme, it will cause them to develop perfectionist or conventionalistic behaviors later in life.

Owls are both logical and practical, accumulating information that can be useful. Abstract thinking is not natural and they do not indulge in romantic or idealistic visions. These people have RRSPs for themselves as soon as they start work and RESPs for their children soon after their offspring are born. Sometimes they actually purchase a home before they get married and pay off the mortgage prior to having children.

Owls learn by adapting and integrating what is being communicated into complex, but logically sound, theories. They think problems through in a step-by-step and pragmatic manner. They tend to come across as perfectionists, who will not rest easily until things are tidy and fit into a rational scheme.

Owls are interested in basic assumptions, principles, theories, models and systems. Their philosophy is: "If it is logical, it is right." Questions they frequently ask include, "Does this make sense?" and "How does this fit with that?"

Although very sensitive to other individuals, Owls will come across as detached, analytical and dedicated to objectivity rather than anything approaching subjective, ambiguous or touchy-feely. Their approach to problems is consistently logical. This is their "mindset" and they rigidly reject anything that does not fit with it.

When sleeping, Owls prefer to lie on their stomachs with their arms up by their heads. They tend to gravitate to a lifestyle of condominium living in an urban setting where they can eat out, travel, shop, attend theatre, musicals and social events.

They will usually plan their vacations well in advance and select organized tours of cities and countries. They will attend museums, galleries, cafés and concerts in the hope of learning of new things.

Their office will have an air of conservatism and have all the tools for working, such as a clock, wall chart, whiteboard, graphs, a barometer, and at the very least a desk organizer. They adhere to their "to do" lists religiously and usually have one for work, one for home and sometimes others. We actually have met one that had a list of their "to do" lists!

Owls are logical and very self-disciplined. They easily assimilate information accurately. They focus on quality and admire people with high standards regarding their work and life. Their opinions are well-thought-out and they make decisions primarily based on facts. They have a knack for problem solving and manage their time well. They are analytical and patient and come across as calm and rational, even though, internally, they may not be. They prefer a task-oriented environment and pride themselves on being precise and accurate. They are most comfortable when there are rules or guidelines to follow.

Owl weaknesses include getting stuck in an either/or mindset and they do not like getting involved in emotional or sensitive situations. They come across as impersonal, even though they are very person-able. It is common for Owls to lose sight of "the big picture." They avoid confrontation, taking risks or making fast decisions. In critical sit-uations they will put right vs. wrong ahead of other people's feelings.

They are not usually team players and can become defensive when criticized. They have a view of certain standards and strive to meet those whenever possible.

When communicating with an Owl, you must be thoroughly pre-pared and provide lots of accurate detail in a persistent, but relaxed, manner. Focus on what you want and why you want it. Prior to con-cluding a conversation, you should check for clarity of understanding.

Owl-Doves

The Owl-Doves with Eagle strengths like to feel safe and secure. When reaching for a goal they make sure they can achieve it; other-wise they will not reach for it at all. Their homes are their most val-ued possessions, along with everything contained within them.

They will not indulge in any pleasure if it jeopardizes the stability and security of home and family life.

Their view of love is that it belongs within the family unit, and even if it is lacking there, they will not compensate for it elsewhere. They like the comfort of culture and tradition, and enjoy friends and family. As peace-loving individuals, they dislike violence.

Owl-Doves can be counted on to be reasonable and logical in living situations, and will compromise in order to satisfy others. Their thought and action is based on what they believe is practical. They rarely act on emotion alone, and quite often feel that they live a dull existence.

When Owl-Doves have Peacock dominance, they will glamorize love interests and home situations so that these objects become their source of pleasure and a means to satisfy their need for security. These people are even less ambitious and competitive than their related combinations, and will not struggle for fame or worldly gain beyond what is required for comfortable living. They enjoy simple pleasures, which are easily accessible.

Owl-Eagles

Owl-Eagles with Dove leanings will take aggressive action to ensure the security of self and family, and are willing to compete and fight for it. They are intelligent, and their approach to problems is both perceptive and logical. These qualities cause them to act first on reason rather than emotion—making them winners more often than losers. They work hard to provide a good lifestyle for their families.

They believe in authority and discipline in both the home and in business, and are not easily swayed by emotion or hard-luck stories. They do not spend much time dreaming or fantasizing.

Those with Peacock strengths are more imaginative than some of the other types and will add a touch of creative thought to the things in which they participate. They are serious-minded, and intent upon keeping emotions under control. They do not need to have their ego stroked by others, and will seek security and self-actualization from personal accomplishments.

Owl-Peacocks

Owl-Peacocks are not easy people to understand or to live with, because there are two strongly opposing factors guiding them. On one hand they respond to practical reasoning and logic. On the other hand their urge for an exciting and romantic life is strong. Consequently, the conflict causes them internal conflict and stress.

Living a routine existence creates great frustration for them, and they might rebel against the lack of change in their lives. Conversely, they are not always aggressive enough to make these changes in their own lives. Picture an individual who wants to purchase a new home but cannot make the decision to sell the old one or put in an offer on the new one, and you will see Owl-Peacock behavior. Recognition from friends and family and personal creative achievements offer some measure of satisfaction for these people.

Frank Lloyd Wright was an architect with imagination and intense drive. He was an Owl-Peacock with an Eagle's strength. These people have ideas that are constructed on a solid base, even though imagination may sweep them away on wild tangents. They have an ability to put challenge in perspective, and use their imagination to develop practical solutions. We have known people of this combination to make several home moves—from living in the city, to the country, and then back to the city. Their ideal life would be to live in a condo during the week, and have a country home for weekends and summers.

These people are not interested in developing close relationships with other people, because it is not a source of pleasure for them. Owl-Peacocks admire others who demonstrate high values. Their desire would be to be able to balance the real world and their dreams.

Flying on Your Own

Once you have learned the strengths and the weakness of each of these birds, and how to instantly recognize them, you will be able to adapt your communication style to be more effective when dealing with them. Understanding these differences will also mean that, from now on, you will be able to appreciate and like almost everyone you meet. You will be able to understand their differing needs and styles. And it is a given that people are just different.

The knowledge of the birds will also enable you to understand how people may behave at work, at social functions, how they approach risk-taking, how they will likely respond to certain stresses, how to approach them in a sales or even relationship situation, and how to deal with them as customers.

Communication is all about understanding and being understood. Familiarity with the nature of these birds will provide the insights to help you understand and be understood by others—a healthy and happy situation from any perspective.

Rules for Team Communications

Leader:

1. Speak for yourself. Do not assume that you can read another's mind.
2. Keep to the point. If you go on and on, people will stop listening.
3. Stop and check with the listener for understanding. Allow them an opportunity to paraphrase what you say.

Team Members:

1. Paraphrase. What do you think you heard the speaker say?
2. Focus on the message, not on what you think the message should be.

Leader and Team:

1. Whoever is speaking is always provided the courtesy of concluding his or her remarks without interruption.
2. The speaker then maintains control of the conversation while confirming understanding with listeners.
3. The leader facilitates equal time for all participants so that no one dominates the discussion.

What Is Your Listening IQ?

The first step to improving any skill is to determine your current skill level. You need to have a measurement of your ability before you can develop a strategy on how and what to improve. After reading each question, give yourself a score of one to five. When you finish, add up your score and review the results

Never		Sometimes		Always
1	2	3	4	5

1. Do you like to listen to other people talk? _____
2. Do you wait until the speaker has finished a complete thought? _____
3. Do you look at the speaker when listening? _____
4. Are you able to ignore distractions? _____
5. Do you stop what you're doing and concentrate fully on the speaker? _____
6. Are you able to put yourself in the speaker's place? _____
7. Do you ask questions to make sure you understand? _____
8. Do you restate what was said to show you got the meaning right? _____
9. Do you encourage the speaker to talk by smiling and nodding? _____

10. Do you hold off judging or criticizing the speaker's ideas? _____

11. Are you aware of certain words and phrases that trigger your emotions? _____

12. Are you able to stay calm when the speaker expresses a concern or problem? _____

Enter your total points here: _____

Results

40 or above: Congratulations. You practice good listening skills. You are also contributing to a healthy workplace. Continue to improve your skills and you will experience even fewer misunderstandings in your relationships. You will also improve your own emotional and physical health.

Below 40: Review what listening skills you do well. Determine what other listening skills you could learn, and determine which of these you would be willing to practice and improve. Every time you increase your listening skills you are contributing to a healthy workplace. Listen to others, and you will be listened to.

Add your own: There may be other listening skills that you practice that are not described in the previous exercise. Any listening skill that improves understanding will make your relationships better. Feel free to list these skills below. Score these skills and add the points to your results.

My listening skills examples:

_____

_____

_____

_____

_____

Conflict

Assert Harmony Through Collaboration

Men are disturbed not by things, but by the views which they take of them.
Epictetus, Greek philosopher, first century AD

Harmony Through Conflict

Conflict in the workplace is very common and healthy. The way people deal with conflict is the factor that will make the difference between positive working relationships and a negative environment. Unfortunately, there is a common assumption that people naturally know how to work together in harmony. This belief has caused the failure of many organizations to effectively implement the empowered team concept.

Fortunately, however, we now know that working together in harmony does not come naturally for most people. Many hold on to the belief that people will naturally come together and work for the good of the group, but our experience has shown us just the opposite. Leaders need to know that working together is a skill that must be learned.

Why People Differ

There are many reasons at the root of conflict. People differ on what the problem is, what the facts are leading up to the cause of the problem, and what the most appropriate methods and processes should be to resolve the problem. Individuals bring different skills to the table, and as a result will look at the problem from different perspectives.

Reasons behind conflict also include the fact that people differ on what should be the most appropriate leadership style to manage the situation. Differences may also occur when our personal goals differ from the organization's goals. To have a healthy workplace, we know that each employee must be getting their personal goals met; and to complicate matters further, every employee will have a different set of personal goals.

Additional causes for conflict are what we call the "belief systems." We know that individuals operate from a different set of personal values, or a different priority ranking on those values. People are all motivated differently. Add to that the fact that communication, thinking and decision-making styles may differ. As well, most people desire harmony in a conflict situation. Everyone has their own focus on how that harmony should be achieved. For those who wish to pursue the 'ins' and 'outs' of individual differences, other chapters of this book cover them in more detail.

Creating Harmony

Strange, isn't it? We never say: "Let's have a rectangular-table discussion." But "round-table discussion" has become a part of normal business language, and there is more than furniture and symbolism involved.

A round table is free of corners, and a good leader wants conversations to flow, free of obstacles or barriers. In fact, round tables are known to encourage participation and remove distinctions between members.

In trying to create harmony with others, some of us act in ways that are quite assertive—even with the best intentions. Others behave in ways that are less assertive. Some people try to achieve harmony by being as cooperative as they can. Others are not so cooperative.

People who are assertive and not cooperative are said to be people who compete. If they compete, team members feel that it is important for them to win. We know that competing and winning will not bring harmony to the team, or the best solution for that matter.

Assertiveness without cooperation is aggressiveness.

Some people behave in ways that are very cooperative and not assertive—in short, they are said to accommodate. We know that when people always accommodate, this will not bring an optimum solution to the team either. Those who are not assertive, nor are they cooperative, are people who avoid. Avoiding issues also never brings you to the best solution.

However, most people have been conditioned to be a little assertive. Some have even taken assertiveness training. Others have been conditioned to try to be a "little" cooperative. Those who are a little cooperative and a little assertive are those people who will tend to compromise. Although there is a belief in the workplace that compromise is good, in fact we find in a team environment, it is the worst. Nobody gets what they want. It is a lose/lose strategy. Even Webster's dictionary defines compromise as: *to settle by making mutual concessions.*

Entrepreneurs do not compromise. Chief executive officers do not compromise. Confident people do not compromise. Great leaders do not compromise.

Assertiveness with cooperation is collaboration. This style alone creates harmony, commitment and a healthy workplace.

Tips for Reducing Conflict

- Be assertive
- Be cooperative
- Use "I" statements
- Focus on the problem
- Keep all comments short
- Focus on specific, alternate solutions
- Avoid criticizing others, especially in public
- Find points on which everyone agrees
- Be honest and open about feelings

It's the Thought That Counts

Let's start with the concept that there is no way another person, thing or event can make you mad or upset. The truth is no external situation, not even your boss or co-workers, can get you angry, upset or distressed. *You upset yourself.*

Now we realize that's a pretty strong statement. Clients have been known to disagree with us for saying it. Even so, it is true. If you disagree, perhaps you will stick with us while we expand on the idea.

Even as authors in the area, we will admit that years ago we would also have blamed somebody else when we got upset. Since then, however, we have learned that we all have the power to deal with our conflicts and anger in constructive ways.

"How do I get *myself* so upset?" you may ask. The answer is always the same: "Through your own *thinking,* your belief system, and your own point of view." It is our *thinking* that determines our *feelings* and *actions.*

The idea is an old one. Epictetus may have been one of the first to illustrate this concept. Some centuries later, Shakespeare reminded us about it again when he wrote in *Hamlet*: "There is nothing either good or bad, but thinking makes it so."

Clearly, people have realized it for centuries, even millennia; even so, as human beings, we often like to ignore the facts. Besides, it is so much easier to blame somebody else and make them responsible for our anger. Not necessarily right, or useful, but easier.

Nevertheless, the powerful truth is that your beliefs create your reality. What you believe about an event will determine how you respond to it. Human beings have the unique capacity and ability to think and reason, and that's why it happens. According to several experts—Albert Ellis, Aaron Beck and Donald Meichenbaum, among others—self-talk plays an important role in our coping skills, as does how we get angry and how we fight. Unfortunately, we also have a tendency to use negative self-talk, and it can become automatic over time. When a particular button is pushed, it is as if we have a program in our brain that starts to run. Since the things we say to ourselves about a situation will have a direct result on how we feel and then behave, it is tremendously important that we become aware of our own belief systems and our own programming.

Let us present a brief illustration by using a simple A.B.C. method developed by Albert Ellis. For a detailed description of this method, we recommend you read Dr. Ellis's excellent book, *A New Guide to Rational Living*. This simple system is based on the premise that when **something happens,** such as when your boss criticizes you, that triggers your **attitude** or **belief** about the criticism, which in turn creates your **reaction as a result of your belief**.

A. **Activating event:** Your boss says, "I hate to remind you again, but I'm still waiting for your report."

B. **Beliefs or thoughts:** Your program is activated. "There's that irritating, controlling behavior again. It's just too much. I can't stand it."

C. **Consequence or emotional reaction:** You feel angry or depressed, or even hostile.

It is not the event, but rather it is your interpretation of it, that causes your emotional reaction and consequent behavior.

The more extreme your point of view about what your boss does or says, the more intensely you will feel about it. Before you start thinking that we are suggesting that you suppress your emotions, let's be clear. Rather than advising you to become a computer-like robot, that operates without expressing feelings, we are suggesting the benefit of becoming aware of your emotions, understanding them and learning to deal with them appropriately.

Anger is not something that happens *to* us. It is our own thinking and our own interpretation that creates our reaction. That understanding can be powerful in changing your behavior and your results. So the next time you upset yourself by making a negative interpretation, see if you can identify your negative self-talk. Determine how your thoughts are responsible for your emotional upset. Take responsibility and go to the next step, which is to **dispute** and **question** your negative self-talk. Whenever you can change your thinking, you will always create a **new effect** and **emotion**.

Returning to the previous A.B.C. example, with positive self-talk we can produce a different reaction.

D. **Disputing negative self-talk:** You could say to yourself, "Maybe the reminder was justified. I have been putting it off and I can see that would be frustrating for a manager. Perhaps it isn't controlling, but a realistic request for a report that is needed.

E. **New effect or emotion:** Accepting that your boss has a legitimate concern lessens the anger. Also knowing that the more you resist, the more the pressure for the report will increase, can help you change your thinking, and that will change your reaction.

Even if you know that your boss does not have a legitimate concern, and may even be acting irrationally, you still have the ability to control your reaction through the power of your own thinking. Perhaps it would be useful to reflect on another thought from our friend, the Greek philosopher Epictetus: "If your body were to be put at the disposal of a stranger, you would certainly be indignant. Then aren't you ashamed of putting your mind at the disposal of chance acquaintance, by allowing yourself to be upset if he happens to abuse you?"

A change in mind will result in a change in feelings.

The Self-fulfilling Prophecy

Understanding the power of your own thinking, and knowing how it can affect your behavior, is an important step in dealing with conflict. It is also important to understand how your self-concept, how you see yourself and your expectations, can affect when and how you argue in a disagreement.

Through your own thinking, and what you expect will happen, you can actually affect the outcome of a situation. It is called a self-fulfilling prophecy. You actually do it all the time, especially when it comes to disagreements.

- You anticipate that bringing up a difficult issue will result in a showdown, and your expectation comes true.
- You expect to get angry if your boss reminds you about something you forgot, and you do.
- You say you are not going to like a certain discussion, and sure enough, you don't.

Whenever you believe and predict that something is going to turn out badly, there is a good chance that you make it turn out that way or you help make it happen. Think about a time you had to make a presentation and you said to yourself, "I'm sure I'm going to blow this." How did you feel? Did it give you confidence, or did you end up forgetting things? Most likely it was the latter. Your prediction comes true because your self-concept influences your behavior, and you start doing those old familiar things that lead to the same old familiar outcomes. Henry Ford's well-known saying sums up the idea perfectly. "If you think you can, or [whether you think you] can't, you are right."

I'm sure you have had the experience of seeing a certain look on your boss's face and thinking, "He's going to get upset when I tell him this." Once you have decided on the outcome, you start acting in a way that makes it come true.

Accordingly, use the power of your predictions and turn them into positive expectations. And by that we don't mean saying, "I'm positive he's going to get upset when I tell him this." We mean turning around your negative expectations and self-concept. You may be pleasantly surprised at the results once you start believing that you will have a good outcome from your disagreements. We overemphasize the importance of maintaining a positive outlook for a very good reason. **If you want to break a negative cycle, believing that you can do it is the most important factor**.

The next time you find yourself getting upset or unmotivated after a particularly frustrating disagreement, remember that there is ample evidence that your own thinking and expectation affected the result.

The destiny for each of us begins with a thought. That thought influences how we feel. How we feel determines what we do. What we do on a regular basis determines our habits, and our habits determine our character. Finally, it is our character that ultimately determines our destiny. Clearly, we must be vigilant about what we think.

Those Little Irritants

Have you ever wondered why a simple little irritant can cause a major blow-up? Or something you used to think was cute is now making you cringe? Well, it could be because you are letting little events pile up and accumulate until they have become a major problem. You may be collecting these minor irritants and bottling them up until the pressure gets too much and you explode.

You are not alone. Many people store these incidents away, and save them for something really big. Unfortunately, it usually takes just one more little irritant to lead to a blow-up.

To illustrate the concept, we use the analogy of trading stamps. Many of us collect stamps from various retail outlets to be applied against future purchases, or we accumulate points for air travel. When it comes to conflict we often collect emotional trading stamps.

For example, you might be irritated because your co-worker left an uncompleted report on your desk. You say to yourself, "It's no big deal, I'll just finish it myself and hand it in." Perhaps, it is no big deal, but an emotional trading stamp goes in the book. Sometime later, the same person arrives a few minutes late for an important meeting. Again you think, "Oh well, I won't say anything because they probably have a good reason for being late." Another stamp goes in the book. And it continues, until one day you discover some minor infraction—such as the person borrows something from your office without asking—and you blow up. You go to your book and to your dismay you discover that it's full. Consequently, it seems the only option you have is to cash in. And, boy, do you *cash in!*

How many of you collect and save these kind of emotional trading stamps? Some of them might be labeled guilt stamps, pity stamps or hostility stamps. Maybe you can think of some favorite ones you collect in your business or personal relationships?

The fact is that saving these stamps leads to a repression of your emotions, which when finally released can not only overwhelm you but also the other person. The person receiving this assault may be totally stunned and wonder about the major reaction to such a minor irritant. If they are fortunate enough to catch on that this outburst is being triggered by a whole bunch of small offenses, they may have a chance to understand your anger. However, when the assault is intense, it is extremely difficult for anyone to remain calm and receptive.

It would be better not to wait until you have collected too many offences, and to deal with the ones that bother you in a timely and reasonable manner when you are not upset. Express your concern and share your difficulty in dealing with the person's behavior. Accept that what may be irritating to you is not at all uncomfortable for the other person. In fact, they may have some valid reason for behaving in the manner they do.

Another answer that might prevent a "cashing in" incident would be for the other person to consider adjusting their behavior and thereby diminish the amount of times they commit these little irritants. The first step is to share with them and make them aware of the behavior that is a potential irritant.

If you think that everyone should be aware of the annoying things they do, think again. Too often, we do not see what other people see. We recall doing a number of "mock interviews" when we were performing career counseling. These videotaped interviews were designed to help candidates improve their interviewing skills by reviewing their behavior. It never failed to surprise these candidates when we would stop the tape and ask them if they were aware of their distracting habits. Some were slouching, looking away, tapping fingers, breaking up a Styrofoam cup, or picking at clothing and body parts.

You may not consider any of the behaviors to be "such a big deal." However, it would be better for reducing conflict if you accepted another person's opinion about their difficulty in dealing with these behaviors. If they are truly no big deal, you might consider adjusting your behavior. Conversely, try to do what you can to stop yourself from collecting those emotional trading stamps.

The Blaming Game

The Blaming Game can probably take the prize as the most popular game in the world. The topic requires a bit of extra attention, because too often we are not aware of what we are doing when we become "blamers."

Many of us grow up blaming almost everyone in our lives for our unhappiness. We blame our bosses, our friends, our customers or our suppliers. We then frustrate ourselves further by going out into the world to look somewhere else for happiness. We incorrectly assume that when we find the right boss or company, we will be fulfilled. We may sometimes even envy other workers who appear to be happy and think, "They are only happy because they found the right environment." We become like a cat chasing its tail.

The mistake we make is believing that happiness is external. As soon as we take on this belief, we forget to look inside ourselves for happiness. Then, of course, we are disappointed when our workplace isn't making us happy. And, completely disillusioned, we continue our blaming game.

As adults we are totally responsible for our own attitudes and behaviors.

Another basic truth is that we teach people how to treat us. In our desire to seek recognition, we often let people treat us in any way they choose. When you are being put down or criticized by others, you need to take some responsibility. When you stop letting others put you down, they will stop doing it. It's that simple but, yes, equally as difficult. It takes courage and a good amount of self-confidence to stand up for your rights and say, "I'm not going to allow myself to be treated this way any more." If another person insults you, treats you disrespectfully or puts you down, you are well within your rights to tell them, "If you talk to me like that I'm not going to stay here and listen."

Take responsibility for your own attitudes and behaviors, and stop blaming others for not giving you something that is not in their power to give.

Who Am I and Why Do I Behave This Way?

To create a constructive working relationship, achieve harmony in the workplace and reduce conflict, there are two key players in the process. One is the manager, the other is the individual.

We dealt with the role of managers and their influence on employees' behaviors in Chapter 4, Coaching. In this chapter, we want to deal with how influences such as environment and mental conditioning will cause people to exhibit either appropriate or inappropriate behaviors, due to their thoughts and responses.

Any journey to success, even workplace success, begins with research—in this case, personal, inner questioning. People have to ask themselves, "Who am I, and what causes me to act the way I do?" The answer is key to how successful people will be in their chosen careers, how effective a leader they will become, and why there may be conflict in their lives.

In his book *Manifest Your Destiny*, Wayne Dyer uses the analogy that if you squeeze an orange, you will get orange juice. If your boss squeezes an orange, he or she will get orange juice. If your spouse squeezes an orange, orange juice again! Why? Because that's what is in an orange. It does not matter who puts pressure on it, that is what will come out.

People are the same way. What is in you is in you, and it does not matter who squeezes (puts pressure on) you. What is in you will come out. The key difference, however, is that we can choose what is in us, and change the way we respond when we are squeezed. But first we must know what is in us, why it is there, and then take action to change any of it that results in negative behavior or behavior that is not getting us where we want to go.

Through its many years of research, Human Synergistics® has established significant connections between an individual's health, relationships and career success, and how they have been conditioned to respond to particular stimuli. Then the organization developed the Stylus™, a quantitative instrument that measures 12 sets of behavioral norms associated with three general types of reactionary behaviors.

Every hour, of every day, of every week, we are bombarded with some sort of stimulus. This may come in the form of an event, a situation or an encounter with another person. We have all been conditioned to respond in some way. The response may be either appropriate or inappropriate.

The reason individuals respond differently is directly related to how they think of the event, situation or person. Their thoughts will result in them behaving passively, aggressively or constructively.

Choosing Road Rage or Not

Driving can provide us with a perfect example. You are driving down the highway, listening to the radio, minding your own business and going the speed limit. Suddenly, a black car with tinted windows and a loud engine squeezes by you, causing you to almost go off the road. The driver then forces his or her way in front of you. How do you feel? What do you do? What happens to you physiologically? How do you feel when you arrive at your destination and encounter a co-worker or spouse wanting your attention?

If you are like many people, your heart will race faster, your blood pressure may go up, your gastrointestinal system will increase the secretion of acids. In response, you might ride up on his bumper, blast your horn, try and pass to get in front of him, or at least give him the proverbial finger.

Others might say, "Oh my!" and drive into the ditch to get out of the way, backing off, to the extent that they might even cause someone else to go off the road. Then they would probably be all shook up over the event. Still others might take appropriate action to carefully slow down in order to avoid an accident, consider that they may have been in a blind spot, or even think the driver of that black car might have a valid reason for doing what he or she did.

Now we will tell the story again. Pay careful attention. You are driving down the highway, listening to the radio, going the speed limit and minding your own business. Then the radio announcer interrupts the music and says, "Folks, if you happen to be driving down this particular highway at this particular time, there is a young man in a black car rushing to the hospital. His wife is in the back seat and she is in labor, he is trying to get her to the hospital as quickly as possible. If you…" Suddenly, a black car with tinted windows and a loud engine squeezes by you, causing you to almost go off the road, and forces his way in front of you. How do you feel? What do you do? What happens to you physiologically? How do you feel when you arrive at work or at home and encounter a co-worker or spouse wanting your attention?

Probably your heart rate and blood pressure would not go up, nor would your stomach be upset. You would probably act appropriately on the highway and drive around the situation carefully. You might actually feel a rush of compassion for the young driver. When you arrive at home or work and encounter a co-worker or spouse, your mood would probably be more positive.

Why did you behave differently in each of those situations? Many people will answer, "The facts changed." But they did not. The facts were exactly the same in both situations. The only thing that changed was what you thought of the driver of that car. Yes, you did think differently because the radio announcer had put additional information into your head to help you think differently.

We all have to be conscious of the fact that all our behavior is based on our thoughts. We must realize who really is responsible for putting the information into our head. The answer is each of us. We are responsible for how we think. Therefore, we would be wise to filter and interpret information differently to enable us to behave more appropriately.

Clearly, our little story is only one illustration of the idea that how you think, or interpret a situation, will have long-term effects on your health, relationships and what successes you might reach in your career. To support you in your journey to self-discovery, we have included an overview of the Human Synergistics® Stylus™ that will measure your attitude and behavior against some styles of thought.

The Circumplex is comprised of three categories—Constructive, Passive/Defensive and Aggressive/Defensive—each further broken down into four behavioral styles.

The four Constructive styles include:

Achievement—The achievement scale measures a way of thinking that is associated with developing effectiveness through the process of setting specific measurable goals and working towards them with unbending determination.

Self-actualizing—The score on this scale measures a way of thinking that results in the highest form of personal fulfillment. This thinking is associated with a high acceptance of self.

Humanistic—The scale measures an individual's personal interest in other people and the desire to help others improve.

Affiliative—It measures the degree of commitment to forming sustaining and satisfying relationships.

The four Passive/Defensive styles include:

Approval—This measures the need to be accepted by others to increase self-worth. These people typically try to please everyone but themselves.

Conventional—The score measures people's tendency to act in a conforming way. They focus, for example, on following rules for the sake of following rules.

Dependent—The scale measures the degree to which personal efforts do not matter. This thinking originates in a high need for security and self-protection.

Avoidance—The avoidance scale measures a person's tendency to withdraw in a situation of confrontation. A person thinking in this style will hide their feelings and shy away from situations they find threatening.

The four Aggressive/Defensive styles include:

Oppositional—This style reflects the extent to which a person will disagree with others and seek attention by being cynical and critical.

Power—This scale indicates the extent to which a person associates self-worth with the ability to control others.

Competitive—This scale measures the need to establish a sense of self-worth through competing against and comparing oneself to others.

Perfectionistic—This section measures the degree to which a person feels a driving need to be seen by others to be perfect and to avoid mistakes. The concept of perfectionism, or someone's driving need to have everything absolutely perfect, is not the same as a person who strives for perfection or tries to do his or her best but will accept the outcome even if it is not perfect. They are dramatically different.

We are providing an example of a somewhat dysfunctional profile as measured by the Human Synergistic® Stylus™ report.

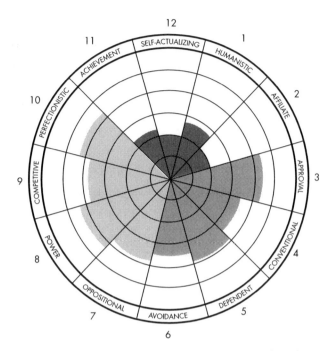

Copyright by Human Synergistics Inc.® Reproduced with permission.

Notice the low scores on the Constructive style, and the proportionally higher ones in the Passive/Defensive and Aggressive/Defensive styles.

A person whose profile has low scores in the Constructive style would have the following issues: From an achievement perspective, they normally do not document or focus on goals, and do not believe that an individual can make a difference. They will try to blame others for their own personal failure, and might shy away from challenging tasks.

A person with low scores in Self-actualization would show a lack of commitment to the organization, would not accept change easily, and would tend to become defensive and depressive when out of their comfort zone.

People with low scores in the Humanistic style normally do not care about growth and development in others, and will tend to focus on themselves. They may avoid healthy conflicts and do not display an interest in serving as a role model for others.

A person who scores low in Affiliative would not be friendly or cooperative towards others, and probably would not accept change readily.

In the Passive/Defensive styles, people with a high score in Approval will tend to set goals that please others, support those with the most authority and try to agree with everyone.

A high score in the Conventional style will be a person who treats rules as more important than ideas and people, and follows policies and practices by the book.

A person who has high scores in the Dependent style will tend to rely on others for direction, be a good follower and will not challenge others.

High Avoidance people react by "laying low" when things get tough, avoiding conflict, and struggling over most decisions.

In the Aggressive/Defensive styles, people who score high in Oppositional oppose new ideas, look for other's mistakes and resist change.

People with high Power scores want to control everything. They believe in using force to get what they want and will seldom admit to their own mistakes. They tend to have very little confidence in other people.

A person with high scores in the Competitive style is the kind of person who competes rather than cooperates and has a strong need to win. They constantly compare themselves to others.

A Perfectionist is the kind of person who never wants to make a mistake, sets unrealistic goals, tries to personally take care of every detail and tends to create self-induced stress.

A more functional profile on the Human Synergistics® Circumplex™ would look more like the following graph.

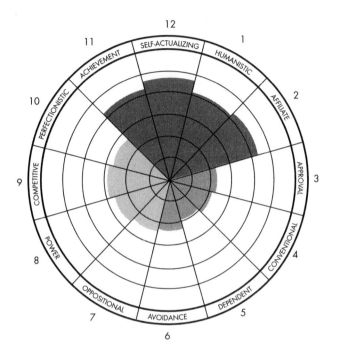

Copyright by Human Synergistics Inc.® Reproduced with permission.

These people would display more positive attitudes and behaviors represented by appropriate scores in each of the three categories.

A person with an ideal Constructive profile and who scores high in Achievement will anticipate future trends and opportunities, take reasonable and well-calculated risks, and will take initiative to get things done. They will try to select team members that will complement the skills of others and are firm in what they believe.

Self-actualized people deal with issues objectively and honestly and stand up for their beliefs. They generate unique solutions to their problems.

Humanistic individuals are sensitive to the needs of others, encourage others to express their ideas, and promote open communication. They motivate others by serving as role models.

Affiliative people get cooperation through personal loyalties. They are charismatic and share personal feelings easily.

People who have appropriate scores in the Approval style are friendly, will accept others' values and rely on their own judgment.

People with low scores in Conventional are not bound by policy and are able to bend the rules when necessary. They are not upset by change but can be tactful when appropriate.

Low Dependent people do not depend on others for ideas. They like responsibility and are capable of taking charge.

Low Avoidance people do not procrastinate, are proactive in problem solving and are willing to take risks.

Ideal Aggressive styles include a low score in Oppositional. These people question decisions made by others, and have an ability to ask tough, probing questions. They do not, however, attack the person.

People who have a low score in Power respect the chain of command, are interested in gaining influence, and expect loyalty from their people.

A low score in Competitive would be people who are realistic about their accomplishments, are persistent and tend to be self-assertive.

People with an appropriate score in Perfectionism would work to obtain quality results, and would have an efficient, businesslike approach to tasks. They would not jeopardize the completion of tasks by demanding perfection.

Completing the LSI™

If you would like to complete one of the LSI™ (*Life Styles Inventory*™), please contact the authors directly by e-mail at: joe@ethos.on.ca or luke@thecouplescoach.com. For further information, these instruments are also available by contacting Human Synergistics® by phone at 519-284-4135 or e-mail: info@hscanada.ca.

LSI™ (*Life Styles Inventory*™). All rights reserved.

What Is Your Conflict IQ?

The first step to improving any skill is to determine your current skill level. You need to have a measurement of your ability before you can develop a strategy on how, and what, to improve. After reading each question, give yourself a score of one to five. When you finish, add up your score and review the results

Never		Sometimes		Always
1	2	3	4	5

1. Do you take responsibility for the outcome of your conflicts? _____

2. Do you accept responsibility for your own reactions, rather than blaming the other person? _____

3. Do you deal with minor irritants before they pile up? _____

4. Do you attempt to deal with all employees' concerns? _____

5. Do you attempt to get all concerns and issues immediately out in the open? _____

6. Do you tell the other person your ideas and then ask for input? _____

7. Do you attempt to work through your differences immediately? _____

8. Do you always lean toward a direct discussion of the problem? _____

9. Are you usually concerned with satisfying everyone's wishes? _____

10. Do you explore alternatives rather than offering a solution? _____

11. Do you always share the problem with the person in order to work it out? _____

12. Do you refrain from making threats and ultimatums? _____

Enter your total points here: _____

Results

40 or above: Congratulations. You practice good conflict resolution skills. You are also contributing to a healthy workplace. Continue to improve your skills and you will experience even fewer misunderstandings in your working relationships. You will also improve your own emotional and physical health.

Below 40: Review the conflict resolution skills you do well. Determine what other skills you could learn, and determine which of these you would be willing to practice and improve. Every time you increase your conflict resolution skills you are contributing to a healthier workplace.

Add your own: There may be other conflict resolution skills that you practice that are not described in the previous exercise. Any skill that improves harmony will make your working relationships better. Feel free to list these skills below. Score these skills and add the points to your results.

My conflict resolution skills examples:

_____

_____

_____

_____

_____

Connection

Be Known...or Be Alone

**The organization which can bring together all
employees and harness their collective potential
will create the most powerful force for
developing long-term, positive growth.**

We believe that one of the most underutilized resources in most
organizations is the potential of their people. The primary
reason for this is the way organizations manage this resource.

The saga begins when we develop high-potential people who
have proven themselves to be very capable of doing their jobs,
whether it's in sales, manufacturing, administration, customer service, or whatever.

We then promote these "doers" to management positions. The
problems begin because instead of doing and fixing themselves, they
must now focus on getting things done and fixing problems through
others. It's a natural progression, since they are so good at "doing."
But the glitch in the system is that they have no experience or training at managing and leading. As a result, they tend to ignore the
development of their people, and burn themselves out trying to be a

"sleeves-up" manager, taking care of every challenge as it comes along.

Today's competitive pressures have forced every organization to re-examine its structure. Most now realize that they can't afford to continue to operate with layer upon layer of management. The following five methods will support organizations in their efforts to succeed in the future:

- Work in a more flexible and flatter structure;
- Have decision making closer to the customer;
- Be obsessed with continuous improvement;
- Maximize the capabilities of everyone within the organization; *and*
- Be faster in creating new ways of doing business.

The Patchwork Quilt

To describe how people must work in the future, and how managers must more often take on the role of facilitator and coach, we are going to use an analogy from the past.

Many of you are familiar with the quilting bee—an age-old North American custom. Interestingly, other countries and cultures also have similar processes and gatherings.

Over the winter months, women who live close to each other would focus on developing, designing and creating the ultimate in beautiful fabric patches. They would invest their skills, their focus, their passion and their high-quality work in each patch to ensure that it was of the highest standards.

Women who had created wonderful patches would then be invited to a quilting bee where they would go to work, making a quilt. If you were a fly on the wall where this was taking place, you would observe some very interesting behaviors.

You would not observe some "boss" quilt lady telling participants where to place their patch, when to take a break, what the rules were, or who should do what task. Instead what you would observe would be all members working in the format of a "team," demonstrating real team behaviors—quite evident by the manner in which they would be working with each other.

They would be communicating with each other, and the communication would be positive. They would be socializing, they would be interested in each other's work, and they would automatically step in to help each other without being asked. But most of all, they would be focused on helping each other look better.

If you continued to observe, when the first woman would put down her patch, the second might come with hers and say, "the colors in my patch bring out and enhance the colors in your patch." Then the third may come with hers and say, "The design in my patch brings together and enhances the pattern in your patches."

Why? They had a vision—to create the most beautiful quilt in the county. To confirm their achievement, they may have entered their creation in the fall fair, with a mission to win a blue ribbon. But whether they did this or not, they all knew there was only one way they could capitalize on each of their talents and create a beautiful piece of art. And that way was to continually help each other look better and support each other to make their work easier.

Our experience with corporations has demonstrated that in order for you to win a "corporate blue ribbon," which may be an employee-of-the-month award or manager-of-the-year award, you had to ensure that other people's "patches," or work, did not look as good as yours. You most certainly were not motivated to help anyone else look better than you.

This is an old, competitive paradigm from the industrial age. And, quite simply, it does not work anymore. Organizations who will succeed in the future are those who see the advantage in having their workforce working in the "quilting bee" model. These organizations will have employees who will sincerely come to work with a mental framework to help each other in their jobs, help others look better and make other people's jobs less stressful.

Think of your own organization. What if everyone in your company came to work each day with one thing in mind? What can I do today to help someone else have a better day? Or, how can sales make administration's job a little easier? How can administration make shipping's job flow better? How can shipping make the sales people's work more productive? And so on.

We are convinced that in the future truly successful organizations are going to be working in this way. In fact, we have already experienced it with some of the clients with whom we have worked. Even in sales functions, they are modifying compensation programs to include what people have done to help others in their work.

Despite the power of this common-sense approach, there are many inhibitors to successfully implementing it in an organization. A major one is our mental conditioning. When most of us started our first job, making our co-workers look good was not high on the scale of how to create future success. In school, sharing work was classified as cheating. With this past conditioning, it will take awhile to change behaviors, and even more time and effort to change the culture.

The other inhibitor or roadblock can be a company's straightforward strategic plan. Companies who want to implement a true teamwork model must have a clearly articulated set of values, a crisp vision that everyone can picture, a detailed mission to which people are committed, and a set of strategic objectives that each employee sees as attainable.

In the 1995 movie *How to Make an American Quilt*, Winona Ryder best articulated how this can be made to work:

> *You must have a theme based on culture. You have to choose your combinations carefully. The right choices will enhance your quilt, the wrong choices will hide original colors and dull their beauty.*

There are no rules to follow. You have to go by instinct, and you have to be brave.

The Right Stuff

In all successful corporate quilts, the composition of "patches" follows a similar mental framework. Then the creation of success comes from the enthusiastic support and teamwork of the employees.

The theme in a company is the stated vision. All employees must be aware of what it is and, more specifically, what their contributions involve.

The culture is based on its fundamental values. These values become the guide to making the right choices and thus create the framework within which all employees must work.

The right choices are based on what the employees believe the mission of the organization to be. A company's mission will determine its priorities, which in turn will lead to the right choices. The right choices will make an organization strong, as evidenced by the experience with Johnson and Johnson during the Tylenol situation.

The wrong choices, even if they appear financially correct in the short term, will make a company weak and cause employees and customers to lose confidence. The Ford Pinto fiasco in 1972, which involved gas tanks that exploded upon rear-end impact, is a perfect example.

In the long term, rules, or bureaucracy, will constipate an organization. Each individual has to know and understand his or her own fundamental values. Personal values provide the framework from which people approach their work. If the employees' values are in harmony with the organization's values, there will be no need for bureaucratic rules. People best realize their potential in an environment that brings out their best.

To be brave, each person must have courage—courage that the organization supports. And we mean not only the courage to succeed but also the courage to fail. Only by experiencing failure will you truly appreciate success. Failure makes people strong, builds character, instills confidence and creates courage.

We have worked with many organizations that have followed this step-by-step process. As a result, they were able to achieve stronger business results and a more positive working environment.

The St. Mary's Story

The media is full of stories of layoffs and closures nowadays, but we have a good-news story derived from some of our Vitamin C processes.

The challenge for the paper mill we are using as an example began in the early 1980s. One of the largest employers in a small, northern Ontario town, it was facing a major dilemma. The mill was part of the Abitibi organization, and those in the head office thought that the mill no longer fit with the long-term growth strategy. As a result, Abitibi decided to close or sell the mill.

A businessman came on board who brought new hope to the mill. He decided he would purchase the mill and run it as a private corporation. Not only did he manage to keep it operating, he also invested heavily in improving the grades of paper which could be produced at this location. He purchased high-speed paper machines and other equipment in order to become a key player in the industry. However, a combination of heavy investing, a soft market and a strong dollar came together and forced the company into receivership.

Fortunately, the employees were not people who gave up easily. They operated the company under the guidance of a bankruptcy trustee while a new owner was sought. All employees and managers agreed to take a 20 percent decrease in pay just to keep it operating, accomplished by a collaboration of employees, management and the unions.

After a year and a half, the firm found a new owner. But the story has a twist. Employees became part owners. Then in October 1994, the new and viable St. Mary's Paper Limited was born, with employees owning about one-third of the mill, an investment firm one half and creditors owning the remainder.

Because of the substantial ownership by employees, there had to be a new management approach, away from the traditional, autocratic management styles normally used in this type of operation. A different operating culture was key. Employees not only shared the day-to-day operations of the mill, but also participated in an open sharing of all critical information, future plans and major decisions.

The new mill manager not only fit the new culture required for success, he also encouraged sharing of internal resources, collaboration and employee involvement. In addition, he took the ideas a step further by focusing on personal development strategies for the management team and the employees.

Through their recent history, the values that had become important to this team included the following:

Respect: Employees will treat everyone with respect by considering each other's opinions, listening to understand, interacting with each other in a rational, open and sincere manner, and appreciating others' contributions.

Involvement: We will show that people matter by appropriately informing and involving everyone in the decisions that affect their work.

Secure future: We believe our future will be secured by managing our assets, suppliers, financial, natural and human resources in such a way that we satisfy our customers and meet our shareholders' long-term expectations.

After much discussion, the **vision** they chose was, "To be the printers' choice for paper."

The chosen **mission** became, "To produce quality paper at competitive costs."

With this in place, these diverse groups connected with the overall plan. As a result, St. Mary's is currently an extremely successful company, surpassing the expectations of everyone who was involved in its creation. After a few years of sacrifice, hard work and commitment, the employees who came together in 1999 were able to enjoy a significant return on their share dividends and a substantial bonus program. In addition, employees who remain loyal continue to enjoy the financial rewards.

The turnaround and success was only possible because management, employees and union members came together. Then they proceeded to work in a way that respected each other's values, developed a spirit of open communication and focused on the desire for a long-term secure future.

The Benefits of Connecting

There are still many organizations that do not see the benefits of having employees connect and form autonomous teams. However, we now have many examples of great results. If senior management will create the right environment, provide the proper training and implement a structure designed to support this environment, they find that teams are a superior way to organize work.

The benefits are diverse and far reaching:

- Teams are more flexible than departments organized in the traditional fashion;
- Employees change their focus from satisfying the needs of higher management to meeting the needs of customers;
- The synergy of connection generates more creative problem solving;

- More commitment and accountability occurs when the team has generated the objectives and solutions;
- When people connect in a team, they tend to build on each other's skills;
- Teams will improve the bottom line.

Executives who question this last point, and ask "how?" can find answers in the following results we have seen with our clients:

- Teams reduce the need for ongoing supervision, resulting in fewer front-line managers and bureaucracy;
- Teams are more focused on serving customers' needs, rather than meeting the internal requirements of the organization— thereby using their energies to the best advantage;
- Teams will implement decisions more effectively if they are not top-down directed;
- Generally, the morale of people connected in a team structure will be higher.

Stages of Connection

We have found that in the stages of group development, there are stages that teams experience on their journey to high performance. The stages mean that individuals will behave differently at different times. These four stages, made popular by Bruce Tuckman, are very predictable and no group can escape the process. The four are known as *forming, storming, norming* and *performing*.

Forming

In the forming stage, the members usually feel some excitement and eagerness at the promise of a new working environment.

Expectations are high and everyone is looking forward to great success. Although there may be some anxiety, the productivity and efficiency of the function will continue to increase at its normal rate.

If the team is in the forming stage, the leader must recognize that members will have a high need for structure and certainty. The best thing the leader can do is take care of some essentials: provide an overall orientation, articulate the vision, create a clear framework within which the group must operate, provide a comfortable non-judgmental environment, clarify why each member is part of this connection, and help each individual clarify their own personal goals.

Storming

At some point after the formation has taken place, teams will then "storm"—a predictable stage that cannot be avoided. If the leader has done everything correctly in the forming stage, a rare occurrence, then the storming can be mitigated to avoid a substantial loss in productivity and efficiency. Also, it may not take as long to go through it. But remember, the stage itself cannot be avoided. It's also worth noting that if it is not handled properly, the storming could go on for months and even cause the disintegration of the team.

Storming happens when people experience disappointment because their initial hopes for the team aren't realized. They might storm about the volume of work, tight time schedules or the frustration of long meetings. They might also storm against each other. Cliques could form, or people might appear to be at cross-purposes with other members. Usually the storming causes a reaction against the leader. The leader has the most power and is the most convenient person to blame for their problems. Some members may even start having private meetings and not invite the leader.

This is the toughest stage, and many times it causes the senior management to disband the team and decide that self-managed teams may be good in concept but they don't really work. While remembering that this is a natural part of a team's development, leaders must respond to the storming with the proper strategies to get through the stage constructively.

The main role of the leader in this stage is to understand that the team needs to 'air' differences and deal with conflict. We have gone into greater detail on this subject in Chapter 6, Conflict. The worst thing to do at this time is to suppress conflict and ask people to start getting along. The leader must take on a facilitator role, stay neutral, not react emotionally, and create a constructive problem-solving process and environment.

When we work with teams, we use non-threatening simulation exercises for members to develop and practice problem-solving skills. We also use 360° feedback instruments to help people better understand how their behaviors and styles are affecting the response of others with whom they must work.

Norming

The next stage of norming will come more quickly if the leader is able to deal with the issues in the storming stage and create an environment of learning and development. Norming is the stage where expectations will be articulated, the degree of empowerment defined, and boundaries explained. This stage also brings with it the proper timing to implement education and training programs and to document a code of conduct for working together.

When this happens, the members will experience an increasing level of satisfaction because they have now solved some major problems and have resolved personal conflicts. The new rules of engagement are now the norms by which they will all conduct themselves.

During this stage the leaders should now start relinquishing control to members, not on the desired outcomes, but on how those outcomes should be achieved.

Performing

If the leader has handled the first three phases correctly, and the team is now working together, they will go into the fourth stage called 'performing'. At this stage the team is now ready to settle down and get to the real work at hand. People will start getting more excited as they see progress and experience positive feelings because they are now working collaboratively. Members know each other's skills, they are sensitive to each other's needs, and there is a codependence or symbiotic relationship and a high confidence in their ability to accomplish objectives.

Now the leader must be very careful not to try and take back control, dominate or take personal credit for what the team is accomplishing. Management must put in place a system of rewards for positive team behaviors that are conducive to a constructive working environment and positive results.

Getting to this stage is hard work, and no short cuts should be considered! Such detours will only result in failure. If it does happen, however, and you try to get the team back together again, the resistance will be high and an attitude of cynicism will prevail.

On the other hand, going through the stages correctly will result in congeniality between the leader and members of the team. In fact, if the leader has done a really good job in connecting the team, he or she will be able to stop being a leader all the time and this role becomes shared by the various members on certain projects.

In the recent past, thousands of innovative and responsive organizations have learned about the importance of shifting decision making to the lowest possible level in the organization. But that shift cannot happen overnight, and cannot be implemented by bringing the employees together for a free coffee or T-shirt, and hanging inspirational posters on the walls.

The good news is that connecting employees and empowering them is not a vague concept based on a trial and error process.

This is a very concrete formula for sorting out the specific degrees of empowerment for different levels within organizations, and developing a strategy for enabling them to get to a position of positive performance.

Emotional Connection

"It's the heart afraid of breaking that never learns to dance." This simple yet meaningful lyric, sung by Bette Midler in her song "The Rose," speaks to many of us who are afraid to feel. Sometimes we are afraid of how much power our feelings actually have on ourselves and on others. We distrust how our feelings will be interpreted, and are afraid they will be misunderstood. So, instead of opening up and sharing our innermost experiences, we retreat and attempt to hide our feelings. This is especially true of negative feelings like anger, resentment or disappointment. The problem, of course, when we conceal our feelings, is that we will never be able to fully connect with another person.

We realize that many of us have not learned to express our emotions in a genuine way. What has made it difficult for us to express ourselves on a feeling level is the fact that intellectual, analytical and cognitive skills are highly valued in our society, especially in the business world. We learn, and are rewarded for, the appropriate use of logic. As a result, some of us have incorrectly assumed that our cognitive skills should override the expression of feelings. We talk like a computer, choosing our words carefully and keeping our emotions repressed and securely locked inside.

Unfortunately, the lack of timely emotional expression interferes with our ability to achieve a human connection, the kind of connection that is necessary to understand and solve a "human" problem. As John Churton Collins once said, "Half our mistakes in life arise from feeling where we ought to think, and thinking where we ought to feel."

Fortunately, there is light at the end of the tunnel. Ever since Daniel Goleman's book *Emotional Intelligence* gained popularity, the "f" word—feelings—has become more acceptable. Dr. Goleman has lead the charge in convincing the world of work that the most successful business people are those who have "emotional intelligence" (EQ). He has demonstrated the "factors at work when people of high IQ flounder and those of modest IQ do surprisingly well." Goleman has lead the way in proving that being in touch with our emotions helps us to better understand and get along with others. It is encouraging that our society, which has traditionally placed a high value on thinking and independence, is changing. No longer will the expression of emotions and dependence be seen as a lack of strength.

We find it promising to see more and more people in the business community accepting the need to establish an emotional bond. For example, we recently heard an executive recruiter talk about how he makes a decision concerning which candidate he will present to his corporate clients. To our pleasant surprise, he actually insisted that any person who was unable to establish this emotional connection with him would not move forward as a potential candidate. He would only consider them if the person was able to communicate beyond the cognitive level.

When asked how he could tell that this emotional connection existed, he replied that phrases such as "I trust him, I feel good about him, or I like him," came to mind. This executive recruiter went on to describe that for him, and for a growing number of other professional recruiters, it was becoming more of a *feeling of knowing*. His words were: "An experience that only exists as a result of combining what is in my head and in my gut."

For a long time we have suggested that there is more than the measurement of a person's IQ to determine how "smart" a person is. We believe that *intelligence* is the ability to learn, combined with the ability to reason; while *emotional maturity* is the ability to frame your life experiences in a context, which then allows you to behave in a positive and constructive manner.

Our more holistic definition of a "smart" person is:

Someone who solves life's problems by using their intellectual, emotional, inner-spirit and physical talents to the best of their ability, and uses that ability to make powerful connections with other people.

Build Powerful Connections

We began this book by highlighting the fact that we live in a world where knowledge is growing exponentially. We now end it by reminding you that the attachments you form at work can help you to learn, to know and to understand. Take advantage of any and all opportunities and understand that in your work environment, everyone is a learner and everyone is a trainer. Your workplace can be an excellent place for you to expand your knowledge and to contribute to another person's growth. Spread the knowledge and experience that exists inside your organization.

It has long been accepted that successful people learn from other successful people. This way of learning is known as *mentoring* — an age-old concept. It was first recorded in Homer's epic tale, *The Odyssey*, when Homer described how a loyal adviser, Odysseus, had been entrusted with the care and education of Telemachus.

Mentoring is all about finding a trusted advisor who can help determine how things work and why they are the way they are. A good mentor can also show you what is important or unimportant, and what you should or should not do.

In most organizations, mentoring has meant a one-on-one relationship where a senior or more experienced person becomes a wise and trusted counselor. The problem with this traditional method is that one person can rarely provide the kind of support we often require. We may want diversity in what we learn, to be exposed to a variety of leadership styles, to develop lines of succession, and to increase the span of people with whom we communicate. The best way to achieve that is to build mentoring relationships with a number of people. Recognize that mentoring should really be about creating mutual learning opportunities. You can give to, and receive from, a variety of individuals. In other words, begin networking to increase your connections and find the right people. Find the people who can help you and discover how you can help others.

We know that organizations today expect employees to engage in continuous learning and self-development, as well as being flexible and adaptable. **For a healthy workplace, it is absolutely imperative that organizations focus on creating environments where employees can connect with others, and build strong working relationships.**

> *Skill is fine, and genius is splendid, but the right*
> *contacts are more valuable than either.*
> Sir Archibald McIndoe

Bibliography and Suggested Reading

Adler, Ronald; Rosenfeld, Lawrence; Towne, Neil: *Interplay: The Process of Interpersonal Communication,* 4th ed. New York: Holt, Rinehart and Winston, Inc., 1989.

Ashkanasy, Neal M; Celeste P.M. Wilderom; Mark F. Peterson (Editors): *Handbook of Organizational Culture & Climate.* Thousand Oaks, California: Sage Publications, Inc., 2000.

Bandler, Richard and John Grinder: *Frogs into Princes: Neuro-Linguistic Programming.* Moab, Utah: Real People Press, 1979.

Beck, Aaron T: *Cognitive Therapy and the Emotional Disorders.* New York: International Universities Press, 1976.

Belasco, James A. and Ralph C. Stayer: *Flight of the Buffalo: Soaring to Excellence, Learning to Let Employees Lead.* New York, New York: Warner Books, Inc., 1994.

Berne, Eric: *Games People Play.* New York: Grove Press, 1964.

Blanchard, Ken; Sheldon Bowles: *Gung Ho! Turn on the People in Any Organization.* New York, New York: William Morrow and Company, Inc., 1998.

Bolles, Richard Nelson: *What Color is Your Parachute?(2000 Edition).* Berkley, California: Ten Speed Press, annual.

Bridges, William: *Managing Transitions: Making the Most of Change.* Reading, Massachusetts: Addison Wesley, 1997.

Buckingham, Marcus and Curt Coffman: *First, Break all the Rules.* New York, New York: Simon & Schuster, 1999.

Charlesworth, Edward A, and Ronald G. Nathan: *Stress Management: A Comprehensive Guide to Wellness.* New York: McClelland and Steward Ltd., 1984.

Charney, Cy: *The Instant Manager. (Rev. ed.)* Toronto, Ontario: Stoddart Publishing Co. Limited, 2000.

Clemmer, Jim: *Growing the Distance: Timeless Principles for Personal, Career and Family Success.* Kitchener, ON: TCG Press, an imprint of the Clemmer Group Inc., 1999.

Clifton, Donald and Paula Nelson: *Soar With Your Strengths.* New York: Delacorte Press, 1992.

Covey, Stephen: *The 7 Habits of Highly Effective People.* New York: Simon & Schuster, 1990.

Drucker, Peter F.: *Managing in Turbulent Times.* New York, New York: HarperCollins, 1980.

Ellis, Albert and Robert Harper: *A New Guide to Rational Living.* Englewood Cliffs, New Jersey: Prentice-Hall, 1975.

Flaherty, James: *Coaching: Evoking Excellence in Others.* Boston, Mass.: Butterworth-Heinemann, 1999.

Gaylin, Willard: *Feelings.* New York: Ballantine Books, 1980.

Goldberg, Philip: *The Babinski Reflex.* Los Angeles: J.P. Tarcher, 1990.

Goleman, Daniel: *Emotional Intelligence.* New York: Bantam Books, 1995.

Groth, Mardy; Peter Wylie: *Problem Bosses: Who They Are and How to Deal With Them.* New York, NewYork: Facts On File Publications, 1987.

Hargrove, Robert: *Masterful Coaching.* San Francisco, Calfornia: Pfieffer, 1995.

Hay, Louise: *The Power Is Within You.* Carlsbad, California: Hay House, 1992.

Heifetz, Ronald A.: *Leadership Without Easy Answers.* Cambridge, Massachusetts: The Belknap Press of Harvard University Press, 1998.

Jaques, Elliott: *Requisite Organization: A Total System For Effective Managerial Organization and Managerial Leadership for the 21st Century.* Arlington, VA: Cason Hall & Co., 1996 (2nd Edition).

Kaye, Beverly and Sharon Jordan-Evans: *Love'Em or Lose'Em: Getting Good People to Stay.* San Francisco, California: Berrett-Koehler Publishers, Inc., 1999.

Lankton, Stephen R: *Practical Magic: The Clinical Applications of Neuro-Linguistic Programming.* Cupertino, California: Meta Publications, 1979.

Maltz, Maxwell: *Psycho-Cybernetics.* Englewood Cliffs, N.J.: Prentice-Hall, Inc., 1973.

McGregor, D: *The Human Side of Enterprise.* New York: McGraw-Hill, 1960.

McRae, Brad: *Negotiating And Influencing Skills: The Art of Creating and Claiming Value.* Thousand Oaks, Calif.: Sage Publications, Inc., 1998.

Mehrabian, Albert: *Nonverbal Communication.* Chicago: Aldine-Atherton, 1972.

Naisbitt, John: *Global Paradox.* New York, New York: Avon Books, 1994.

Nelson, Bob: *1001 Ways to Reward Employees.* New York, New York, Workman Publishing, 1994.

Olive, David: *Just Rewards: The Case for Ethical Reform in Business.* Markham, ON: Penguin Books, 1988.

Pavelka, Joe: *It's Not About Time! Rediscovering Leisure in a Changing World.* Carp, Ontario: Creative Bound, 2000.

Secretan, Lance: *Managerial Moxie: The 8 Proven Steps to Empowering Employees and Supercharging Your Company.* Rocklin, California: Prima Publishing, 1993.

Selye, Hans: *Stress Without Distress.* New York: Lippincott, 1980.

Sharma, Robin S.: *The Monk Who Sold His Ferrari: A Spiritual Fable About Fulfilling Your Dreams and Reaching Your Destiny.* Toronto, Ontario: HarperPerennial, 1998.

Sinetar, Marsha: *Do What You Love, The Money Will Follow: Discovering Your Right Livelihood.* New York, New York: Dell Publishing, 1987.

Stein, Steven J. and Howard E. Book: *The EQ Edge: Emotional Intelligence and Your Success.* Toronto, Ontario: Stoddart Publishing Co. Limited, 2000.

Wall, Bob; Mark R. Sobob; Robert S. Solum: *The Mission-Driven Organization*. Rocklin, California: Prima Press, 1999.

Watson, David and Roland Tharp: *Self-Directed Behavior*. Third Edition. Monterey, California: Brooks/Cole Publishing Company, 1981.

Keep in Touch

Dear readers, we are firmly convinced that if you practice the seven "C"s illustrated in this book, you will have a healthy workplace. In fact, we'd welcome your success stories. Let us know how our book has influenced you.

We appreciate you sharing your experience, even though we may not be able to respond to each of you personally.

You can contact us by e-mail at <u>luke@thecouplescoach.com</u> or <u>joe@ethos.on.ca</u>. or by fax at (613) 727-4829 or (905) 473-9725. You may also send comments to Luke De Sadeleer or Joseph Sherren c/o Creative Bound Inc., Box 424, Carp, Ontario, Canada K0A 1L0.

For information about presentations, workshops, special events and products, log on to our Web sites: <u>www.thecouplescoach.com</u> or <u>www.ethos.on.ca</u>.

Creative Bound Resources

a division of **Creative Bound Inc.**
Resources for personal growth and enhanced performance
www.creativebound.com

A speakers bureau with a unique offering! Our speakers are published experts in a variety of lifestyle areas, including stress control and life balance, motivation, leadership development and enhancement of personal and professional performance. They deliver their message in an upbeat, entertaining and accomplished fashion. Presentations are tailored to the needs and goals of each group for optimal impact.

Joseph Sherren and **Luke De Sadeleer** are proven workshop facilitators and keynote presenters. They are available to speak on a variety of topics relating to *Vitamin C for a Healthy Workplace.*

To receive a complimentary information package,
including our **Guide to Products and Services,**
please contact Creative Bound Resources at **1-800-287-8610**
or by e-mail at resources@creativebound.com

Some of our titles:

*Vitamin C for a
Healthy Workplace*
Luke De Sadeleer and
Joseph Sherren
0-921165-73-0
$21.95 CAN $17.95 US

*SHIFT: Secrets of Positive
Change for Organizations
and Their Leaders*
Janice M. Calnan
0-921165-74-9
$18.95 CAN $15.95 US

*Vitamin C for Couples:
Seven "C"s for a Healthy
Relationship*
Luke De Sadeleer
0-921165-68-4
$18.95 CAN $15.95 US

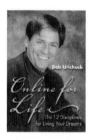

*Online for Life:
The 12 Disciplines for
Living Your Dreams*
Bob Urichuck
0-921165-65-X
$19.95 CAN $15.95 US

*It's Not About Time:
Rediscovering
Leisure in a Changing
World*
Joe Pavelka
0-921165-69-2
$21.95 CAN $17.95 US

*Up Your Bottom Line:
Featuring the ABC, 123
Sales Results Systems*
Bob Urichuck
0-921165-72-2
$21.95 CAN $17.95 US

CREATIVE BOUND INC.

Resources for personal growth and enhanced performance
www.creativebound.com